AWAKEN
THE WRITER
WITHIN

If you want to know how…

Creative Writing
How to unlock your imagination, develop your writing skills – and get published

'This is a book which merits a place on every writer's bookshelf.'
– Writers' Bulletin

Ideas for Children's Writers
A comprehensive resource book of plots, themes, genres, lists, what's hot and what's not

An invaluable resource book with lists of attributes, plots, themes, genres, and locations, and advice on how much description to use.

Write and Sell Your Novel
The beginner's guide to writing for publication

'An excellent introduction for the new novelist.' — Writing Magazine

howtobooks

Send for a free copy of the latest catalogue to:

How To Books
3 Newtec Place, Magdalen Road,
Oxford OX4 1RE, United Kingdom
email: info@howtobooks.co.uk
http://www.howtobooks.co.uk

AWAKEN
THE WRITER
WITHIN

A SOURCEBOOK FOR RELEASING YOUR CREATIVITY
AND FINDING YOUR TRUE WRITER'S VOICE

C A T H Y   B I R C H

3RD EDITION

howtobooks

Published by How To Books Ltd,
3 Newtec Place, Magdalen Road,
Oxford OX4 1RE. United Kingdom.
Tel: (01865) 793806. Fax: (01865) 248780.
email: info@howtobooks.co.uk
http://www.howtobooks.co.uk

First edition 1998
Second edition 2001
Reprinted 2002
Third edition 2005

British Library Cataloguing in Publication Data
A catalogue record for this book is available from the British Library

Cover design by Baseline Arts Ltd, Oxford
Produced for How To Books by Deer Park Productions, Tavistock
Typeset by PDQ Typesetting, Newcastle-under-Lyme, Staffs.
Printed and bound in Great Britain by Cromwell Press Ltd, Trowbridge

NOTE: The material contained in this book is set out in good faith for general guidance
and no liability can be accepted for loss or expense incurred as a result of relying in
particular circumstances on statements made in the book. The laws and regulations are
complex and liable to change, and readers should check the current position with the
relevant authorities before making personal arrangements.

Contents

List of Illustrations

Preface

'The main struggle people have with creativity is that they stop
themselves from doing what comes naturally.'

(Clarissa Pinkola Estés: The Creative Fire)

You know the feeling. You have an idea that just might work. It begins
to take shape in your mind. Excitement grows. You pick up your pen
or sit down at your keyboard and you freeze. Or you begin, and hours
later you are still re-writing the same few sentences and the energy has
gone. Why? Could it be fear of 'getting it wrong'? Remember how
freely you created as a child; how you sang, danced, painted, created
amazing stories and fantasy worlds to play in with your friends – all
for sheer enjoyment, with no anxieties about being 'good enough'.
Close your eyes for a moment and remember how your creativity
flowed.

If you long to write with that sense of spontaneity you had in childhood, this is the book for you. Its wide variety of exercises and
visualisation techniques will enable you to explore the treasures of
your subconscious, revisit your childhood world of games and make-
believe and bring back what you find. Its practical advice on all aspects
of the writing process will enable you to share these experiences with
others through your work.

This book will help you at every stage. Its aim is to get you writing,
keep you writing, and enable you to enjoy your work to the full. Use it
to rediscover your love of words, find your voice and become the writer
you were meant to be.

Cathy Birch

1

Writing – A Way of life

This book is designed to stimulate and sustain your creative flow. It will help you through those difficult patches when inspiration seems to have deserted you, and the whole process feels like horribly hard work. It will help you celebrate and utilise to the full those exciting times when your creativity seems to take on a life of its own and you feel as though you are running to keep up with it. It will enable you to tap into that inner wealth you may have forgotten you had. If you can just remember to have this book to hand and turn to it when needed, you need never be stuck again.

First, the more practical matters. This opening chapter looks at how our work habits can be improved in order to free and maintain that natural creative flow. Management of our time and our resources – including that most important of writers' tools, the human body – is considered as part of this process. Antidotes are suggested for some of the unnatural mental and physical practices we impose on ourselves in order to write. If you feel tempted to skip this section in order to get down to writing straight away, then please remember to return to it later. This is very important. Many writers have found solutions to long-standing problems by taking some of the simple steps suggested here.

WRITING IS A PHYSICAL ACTIVITY

A writer is like an athlete; a *competitor or skilled performer in physical exercises*, to quote the *Concise Oxford Dictionary*.

Because we spend so many hours seated at our desks, it is easy to forget this – until our body protests. Our neck shoulders and head ache, our eyes refuse to focus, our wrists succumb to repetitive strain syndrome, and then we remember that our mind operates through a physical organ in a physical body with needs of its own.

These aspects of a writer's physical make-up need particular attention:

- the brain
- the eyes
- digestion
- joints, muscles, heart and lungs.

Keep your brain alert

Like all our bodily organs our brain needs nourishment, a rich blood supply, plenty of oxygen and adequate rest in order to function well. Hours of sitting hunched in a stuffy room, skipping meals or eating junk food will put it at a disadvantage.

The simple acts of opening a window, circling your arms and breathing deeply will boost mental processes tremendously. If you find it hard to remember to do these things, write a note to yourself and place it where it will catch your eye from time to time.

Brain food

Our brains thrive on foods rich in iron, phosphorous and the B vitamins (particularly B6, which is said to help with 'writer's block'). Liver, fish, pulses, grains, wholemeal bread and green vegetables are all excellent writers' foods. My current favourite 'boosts' are extract of malt, or thick wholemeal toast with tahini, banana and honey. Oh no? OK – what's yours?

Brain fatigue

We need rest, not only to combat tiredness but to enable the body to replenish its cells – which, of course, include our brain cells. For this reason, burning the midnight oil (a common symptom of 'writing fever') may reduce our mental and physical efficiency over time – something we may find it all to easy to forget or ignore. Many writers have found it beneficial to replace their late night writing habit with an early morning start when the world is just as quiet and their brain is rested.

Efficiency is also improved by a regular change of task – on average, every hour and a half. (See glossary: *Circadian rhythms*). Use a timer with an audible signal as a reminder to take regular breaks. Ideally, leave the work room and do something physical. Have a list of suggested activities to hand – anything from a short-duration household task to a brisk walk around the block. Physical movement will invigorate your body. Also it can, in itself, trigger a flow of words and ideas (see *Use physical activity to stimulate your creativity* below).

Brain waves

Your list could include some of the audio-visual products which use pulses of light and/or sound to alter brainwave patterns. A 15-minute session with one of these can calm an agitated brain, or revitalise a flagging one.

Highly recommended are the products available from *LifeTools,* and the light and sound machines from *Photosonix* and *Novapro* (see *Useful addresses*).

Further information can be found via the Internet (see *Personal Growth products and websites*) **NB Pulsing lights should not be used by people suffering from epilepsy.**

Further suggestions for activity breaks appear in the sections which follow.

Checklist

To function well your brain needs:

- ◆ nourishment
- ◆ oxygen
- ◆ rest and relaxation
- ◆ a well-exercised body
- ◆ regular breaks.

Keep your eyes healthy

Computer users

If you use a word-processor, you probably spend many hours staring at the screen. An anti-glare screen, either built in or added on, is essential. If over-exposure causes sore or itchy eyes, try bathing them with a cooled herbal infusion of eye-bright and camomile. Your local pharmacy will also carry a number of good remedies for this condition. (Also see *all writers* below.)

Such exposure can leave eyes deficient in Vitamins A and B2, so supplements of these vitamins are advisable. Vitamins C and E also promote eye health.

Alleviate eye and neck strain by having the monitor exactly at eye-level. If necessary, place some blocks underneath it to achieve this. Positioning your feet at the correct height is also important. Ideally both the knee and the ankle joints should be relaxed and should form right-angles.

All writers

Most methods of getting words onto paper involve your eyes in long periods of repetitive activity. They will function better if you take regular time out to exercise them. Add this 'eye-gymnastics' routine to your activities list. It need only take a minute once you have mastered it.

◆ Hold an upright pencil about 10 cms from the bridge of your nose. Focus on something distant, then focus on the pencil. Repeat several times.

◆ Move the pencil up, down, from side to side and make slow circles with it. Follow these movements with your eyes. Repeat several times.

◆ Without the pencil, repeat the above movements several times very slowly.

◆ Finally, rub your palms together briskly, then cup them over your eyes.

Cold tea-bags, cucumber slices or diluted lavender oil on a damp cloth are all very soothing when laid on closed eyelids. You can also bathe your eyes with a cooled herbal infusion of eye-bright and camomile (as advised for PC users).

Eat well

A tight schedule might tempt you to skip meals, eat junk food, or eat absent-mindedly while still writing. These are false economies which you will pay for in brain and body fatigue – and probably digestive disorders, later. Keeping going with stimulants such as alcohol, coffee and tobacco will also have a punishing and detrimental effect on your system.

You owe yourself proper meal breaks – relaxing times spent *away from your desk*, rewarding mind and body for the hard work they have done. How would you feel about a boss who insisted you work through your lunch hour? Don't do it to yourself!

Exercise your joints, muscles, heart and lungs
How would you feel if ordered to sit in one spot for several hours moving only your fingers? Writers regularly submit their bodies to such torture. The long-term results will be stiff joints, atrophied muscles and a variety of other ills which could adversely affect your life – not to mention your creative output.

To redress the balance, add a choice of physical work-outs to your break-time activities list. Work with a yoga or pilates video for example, to ensure that your whole body is exercised and flexibility and strength are maintained. You also need an aerobic activity, to exercise heart and lungs and send blood and oxygen to all vital organs, including the brain. Jog, cycle, walk your dogs, dance to Gabrielle Roth, work out with Jane Fonda – whatever you enjoy the most.

Tae Bo is a particularly good work-out for writers as it thoroughly exercises the heart, lungs, arms and upper body and brings an invigorating flow of blood to the brain.

The need for desk workers to take regular exercise breaks has long been realised by companies such as RSIGuard, WorkPace, and PrimeMover, who have produced software which interrupts your computer use at chosen intervals and takes you through a work-out, including eye exercises. The websites of such companies are well worth a visit and many offer 30-day free trials of their software. Despite my initial irritation at being interrupted every hour, I have found my health has benefited hugely since I installed one of these programs.

Checklist
Your physical health and, as a result your writing, will benefit from:

- good eye care
- eating well
- sleeping well
- breathing deeply
- taking regular breaks
- exercising.

Use physical activity to stimulate your creativity
As mentioned earlier, physical activity can often release a flow of words and ideas. This could be connected with our early development, as we learn to use the rest of our bodies before we speak. I saw a striking example of this effect while working on a language-skills programme for children with special needs. The group included an extremely withdrawn eight-year old boy who had been silent throughout his three years at school. Having marched round the hall to music, the children wanted to 'march' lying down. As they did so, the boy in question began moving his arms and legs faster and faster against the floor. Suddenly out came a torrent of speech, which increased in speed and volume until he was shouting whole sentences. Somehow that particular sequence of movements had triggered his speech processes.

Using physical triggers to stimulate the thought processes
Practitioners of therapies like Gestalt and Bioenergetics utilise such physical triggers as enabling mechanisms. Writers can do the same. Crawling, kicking, jumping, punching cushions – 'marching

lying down', can all help words to come. Close the curtains and try it – what can you lose!

Writers use a variety of physical triggers to get the creative juices flowing. Veteran sci-fi author Ray Bradbury used to swim. Charles Schulz, creator of Peanuts, would walk or skate. Poet and author Diana Gittins leaps into a boat and rows. Comedy writer Peter Vincent 'gets up from his desk every hour or so to do yoga.' ('Or eat a biscuit,' he adds after some reflection.)

Like many writers, Peter finds that when ideas start flowing he strides about consuming large quantities of food. He also experiences a strong link between his creative process and his physical well-being. He can suffer indigestion and abdominal pain for no apparent reason, make an alteration to the script he is working on and immediately feel fine again – literally a gut reaction.

Checklist
- How does writing affect your body/behaviour?
- What physical activities help you to think better?

Value your health and treat your body well. It is the vehicle of your talent.

Flex your writing muscles
'Get in action,' Natalie Goldberg advises. Work it out actively. Pen on paper. Otherwise all your thoughts are dreams. They go nowhere. Let the story move through your hand rather than your head.'

If writing is your main occupation, you probably write daily from necessity. If not it is good to keep the 'writing muscles' flexed in this way. With any discipline, leaving it for a day can lead to several days and so on – until suddenly weeks have passed and you are horribly out of practice. If the discipline in question is an important part of your life, you can also find yourself horribly 'out of sorts' if you don't pursue it. Writing is no different in this respect. You must maintain the momentum for progress to be made and – if writing is your passion – for well-being to be maintained.

Find the time

When we work from the creative rather than the logical mind, the process cannot be rushed. To derive maximum benefit from the exercises in this book, you need to allow enough time for the experiences to unfold.

However, if you find yourself juggling a heap of responsibilities and wondering how you can possibly clear a space for writing, a short regular slot each day is a good compromise solution. Even if you can only manage ten minutes, at the end of the week you will have 70 minutes-worth of writing under your belt. While not ideal, it keeps you writing. In fact a novel per year can be produced in this way.

CASE STUDY

Karen, one of my students, set herself that very task. She has two young children and works part-time as a computer programmer. As a teenager, she wrote short stories and poetry. For years she had been trying to find time to do this again, but somehow it had never happened. After discussing this in class she agreed that ten minutes a day would be considerably better than nothing. She decided to spend ten minutes of each lunch-break writing (in her car to make sure she was not disturbed). She used an old A4 diary for the purpose and filled a page each day. By the end of six months she written over 80,000 words, which she is currently crafting into a very promising novel.

Go for it

One of the problems with only having ten minutes, is that it can take that long just to start thinking. The answer – don't think. Set yourself a time of ten minutes, twenty minutes, an hour – whatever you have available, and just write. Get in action. Keep your hand moving. Whatever comes; no thinking, crossing out, rewriting – just *do* it. Stick to the allotted time – no more, no less. A timer with an audible signal focuses the mind wonderfully. Some of what you write may be rubbish – fine! When you give yourself permission not to be perfect, things start to happen. You can find yourself swept up in the joy of what writer Chris Baty (founder of National Novel Writing Month) has termed 'Exuberant Imperfection'. At the end of the week look back and highlight the things you might be able to use.

Another excellent way of both flexing your writing muscles and focusing the mind is to set yourself the task of writing a complete story in – say – 100 words; no more, no less. There is currently a group on the BBC *Get Writing* Website (see Appendix) dedicated to writing 60-word fiction. I have found this a good once-a-week substitute for my daily timed writing. Chris Baty's *Write a Novel in a Month* idea, and Nick Daws' *Write Any Book in 28 Days* are greatly expanded versions of this go-for-it approach.

Get started

Write: 'I remember when . . .' or 'I don't remember when . . .' 'I want to tell you about . . .' 'I don't want to tell you about . . .' 'I have to smile whenever I. . . '

Write about a colour, a taste, a smell, an emotion. Write about a favourite outfit, an embarrassing experience, a holiday disaster, a beloved pet, a dream. Write about what it feels like to have no ideas.

Write: 'If I were a piece of music I would be . . .' or 'The woman on the bus made me think of . . .' or 'The meal I would choose as my last would be . . .'

Open a book or turn on the radio and start with the first sentence you see/hear. If you get stuck, write your first sentence again and carry on.

If you would like to try a more technological approach, writesparks.com offers a quick-start generator which is fun to use, and particularly suited to timed writing. It even provides a space and a timer if you want to time-write on your PC rather than by hand. Also try writingbliss.com which, among a huge variety of writing activities, offers to e-mail you a daily writing task – for free!

If you want to apply timed writing to a larger project – say, completing the first draft of a novel, software available from WriteQuickly.com 'guarantees a book in under 28 days, working for one hour per day'. Nick Daws' CD 'How to Write Any Book in 28 Days' and Chris Baty's book *No Plot, No Problem* make similar claims (see *References, Further reading* and *Useful addresses and websites*).

Find new ways
Whether you are doing timed writing, taking notes or first-drafting, writing in a linear way from left to right is only one of

many choices. Try writing round the edges, starting in the middle, writing in columns, spirals, flower-shapes – whatever takes your fancy. I find linear note-taking of little use for recovering information afterwards.

I prefer to 'chunk' my thoughts (see Figure 1) so that they leap off the page, demanding my attention. I draw a shape around each chunk as I write, to keep them separate. (The doodles come later when I am thinking.) I also like to organise my writer's notebook in this way. When I scatter snatches of conversation, description, and general musings around the page, I find they come together in ways I might not have thought of if I had used linear jotting.

I find coloured paper and pens useful – and fun. They alleviate boredom, evoke a particular mood, and help me organise my thoughts.

Checklist
- Set a time and keep to it.
- Decide how you want to position the words on the page.
- Choose a starting sentence and return to it if stuck.
- Don't stop until the time is up.
- Don't think, cross out, rewrite – just do it.
- Try a workbook or some software for a change of approach.

Timed writing as a daily practice
Many writers, whatever their situation, find daily timed writing useful. If short of time, it can help bypass any panic engendered by a blank sheet of paper and a ticking clock. When time is not a problem, it can help combat that perverse ailment, *don't want to start.* Having moved mountains to clear a day – or a life – in which to write, some of us are suddenly afflicted with a paralysing

Fig. 1. 'Chunked' notes from a story-telling workshop.

torpor. This can be because self-motivation is new to us (see *Organising your work time* below) or because of self-doubt (see *Writing and your identity* below). Timed writing cuts through both by a) giving us something definite to do and b) setting no standards.

Try: 'I am now going to write as badly as I can for ten minutes.'

Timed writing also clears mental 'dross' so that the good stuff can start to flow – like priming a pump. It is the equivalent of a performer's or athlete's warm-up exercises. It can also produce something amazing in its own right.

Keep a notebook by your bed and do your timed writing before even getting up. This is an excellent way to kick-start your writing day.

Checklist
Timed writing can help you:

♦ focus
♦ clear your mind
♦ warm up
♦ get started.

WRITING AND YOUR LIFESTYLE

'To nurture your talent requires considerable discipline, for there are many other good things you will not have time to do if you are serious about your creativity.'

(Marilee Zedenek: *The Right Brain Experience*.)

There are also many not-so-good things which you will not have time to do – or may feel forced to do instead. It's amazing how compelling the laundry or this year's first cleaning of the car can feel when you're having trouble with starting your writing project.

CASE STUDY

Sheila, one of my older students, felt she had hit a long-term 'creative low'. She had written with some success in the past, having had several stories published in women's magazines, and a play accepted for radio although it was never performed.

She wanted to write again, but found her days too broken up with various activities to really marshal her thoughts. She told me that since her children had left home, there seemed to be increasing demands on her time.

It transpired she was a school governor, served on three committees, sang in a choir, and did volunteer work in a hospital. Smiling, she admitted that much of this frantic activity was probably a response to the 'empty nest' syndrome. Then she said that recently she had begun to wonder whether she was also using it to avoiding writing in case she could no longer do it well enough.

How important is writing to you?
List all your current projects and activities. Rate the significance of each one on a scale of 1–10, then list them again in order of importance.

◆ Where does writing come on this list?
◆ How does this affect the way you feel about your workspace and work time?

Organise your workspace

Do you need silence or do you, as Peter Ustinov did, find it unbearable? Do you need to be free from distractions, or can you work at the kitchen table while your two-year-old plays football with the saucepans? Do you need everything neatly labelled and filed, or do you prefer cheerful clutter? How important is the decor?

- Take a few moments to imagine your ideal workspace – no restrictions.

- Make this workspace the subject of a five-minute timed writing.

- In your present circumstances, how close can you come to that ideal?

- Make this compromise workspace the subject of a second timed writing.

Claim your territory

You may have to share this space with others. How protective do you feel about the area or areas you use?

- How do you mark your boundaries so that others do not encroach on them?

- Are you clear about your needs for space and privacy?

- How assertive are you in defending these needs?

For many of us this territorial aspect of the workspace is very important, and needs addressing. Having to worry that papers might be moved, read, damaged – even accidentally thrown away, is a most unwelcome distraction.

If you have your own work room, are you making full use of the freedom this allows you? Has it occurred to you that you can do *anything you like* in there? For example, writing on the walls and ceiling can be very liberating – perhaps chunking ideas (as in Figure 1). The result feels amazing – like sitting inside your own brain.

◆ Take a few moments to think about ways of using your space more creatively.

◆ Write a list of the things you will do to bring this about.

◆ Take action.

Go walkabout

Having organised your workspace and settled in, make sure it does not eventually become a new rut. Try working somewhere else occasionally – a change of scene can help ideas to flow. Even a different part of the house can feel surprisingly adventurous when you have got used to one particular location.

If you really want to trigger your imagination, try some of the places you chose in childhood – behind the sofa, in a wardrobe, in the cupboard under the stairs. (Does this sound like a daft idea? Would it help to know that at least two well-known and respected authors write underneath their dining room tables?) In an article called 'Where I Like to Write' (*Author's Copyright and Lending Society News, February 2005*) author Carol Lee describes sitting on a polishing box by the fire when writing in her childhood home. She emphasises the importance to her of finding just the right place.

Karen used to write in the garden shed when she was a child, and has done so again on several occasions, to very good advantage. She says that being playful in this way really boosts her creativity.

'People try to become everything except a song. They want to become rich, powerful, famous. But – they lose all qualities that can make their life joyous; they lose all cheerfulness, they become serious.'

(Osho *Morning Contemplation*)

Wanting to be somewhere else

Do you sometimes feel you need to be somewhere else entirely – then if you manage to get there, find it is not right either? Does isolation make you long for company and vice versa? Do you rent a cottage by the sea, and end up writing in a cafe in the centre of town? 'I thought it was only me!' other writers will probably say if you ever confess. It is very likely that this yearning for something we cannot have, is a necessary part of the creative process. Once, when writing a certain story, I felt compelled to stay in a seaside boarding house up north, in winter. The arrangements I had to make in order to do so were considerable. I stuck it for just one day. Now I use my imagination to go where I yearn to go. This is quicker, cheaper and far less disappointing.

Organise your work time

Does your time feel as though it is structured for you, or do you set your own schedule? We have seen how timed writing can help in both situations. We have also looked at scheduling a writing day around regular breaks. If you are used to working for someone else, both self-motivation and time-management may feel difficult at first. The leisure-time writing habit may also be difficult to kick, so that you find you are writing all day every day and exhausting yourself. Is this something you need to change?

Whether you are fitting writing in or fitting other things in around writing, some organisational skill will be needed. As with your workspace, your work time needs to be claimed and marked out in some way. Those around you will need to know any 'rules' that apply to your writing time. If you live alone, make your writing hours known to friends, neighbours or anyone else who might call round. Let the answering machine take all your calls. Place a 'do not disturb' notice on the front door if necessary.

◆ Think about any areas of tension affecting your writing time. How can you reduce these?

◆ Do a five-minute timed writing about the steps you will take to achieve this.

◆ Take action.

Research

Does your schedule allow plenty of time for any research you need to do? How do you feel about research? It need not mean hours spent in the library. Active research, immersing yourself in the place where your story is to be set, is likely to be more enjoyable and will help you to bring the setting to life for your readers. Novelist Marjorie Darke recommends conversing with 'anyone in the locality who can increase my background knowledge.' She also aims to share as many of her characters' experiences as possible. While researching *Ride the Iron Horse*, for example, she took part in a traction engine race. Similarly Peter Vincent spent many hours as a leisure centre user while doing initial research for *The Brittas Empire*, and Canadian writer Jo Davis thoroughly indulged her passion for trains while working on *Not a Sentimental Journey.*

Novelist Alison Harding describes research as 'a sort of radar that picks up on things you need to know and draws your attention to them'. This radar also seems to work subliminally. Alison, in common with a number of writers, has often had the experience of inventing a happening in relation to a certain place, researching the location and finding that a similar event actually occurred there. I have several times invented a name for a character and had someone of that name enter my life shortly afterwards.

Reading

Make sure your schedule also includes plenty of time for reading – particularly the type of material you like to write. In order to be part of the 'writing world', you need to know what is happening in your chosen field. What appeals to you? What is selling? Who is publishing it? A particular joy of being a writer is that you can feel positively virtuous about being an obsessive reader.

Checklist

♦ What do you need in terms of time and space for writing?

♦ How can you best get these needs met?

♦ How will you make this clear to those around you?

♦ What role might your imagination play?

♦ Have you allowed plenty of time for reading and other research?

CASE STUDY

Another student, David, joined one of my classes when he was made redundant from his job as office manager. He had always wanted to write a crime novel, and decided to make positive use of his time at home to do so. He organised his writing day with as much care and precision as he used in running his office. He realised the importance of reading novels in his chosen genre, and set aside a regular time slot for this. He also allowed plenty of time for research. He was not too sure about things like pilates and writing in cupboards, but could see the value of a good health programme. Having set himself up with such meticulous care, he was surprised and quite discouraged, at the difficulty he found in getting started. He says that timed writing – of which he was extrememly sceptical at first – has been a huge help in this respect. David's novel is still 'in embryo' but, with the help of the exercises in this book, he has written two prize-winning short stories meanwhile.

Stay in touch with the rest of the world

One of writing's many paradoxes is that it is an isolated activity through which we reach out to others. It is a way of making our voice heard in the world. So how might the other half of that dialogue be conducted? Joining a group or a class is one very good way. Becoming an active member of some of the many writers' websites (see *Useful addresses and websites*) is another excellent way (but beware, this can also become very distracting!). Reading the papers, watching the news, and conversing with a variety of people can also be helpful.

Do you read your first drafts to other people and value their response – or do you prefer to internalise the energy at this early stage?

Whatever your choice, the most important question is *does it work for you?*

YOUR WRITER'S TOOL KIT

Essential items

Look at – or imagine, your workspace. List the things you simply could not do without. Is yours a Zen-like existence – just a pad and pencil, or is your room overflowing? Would you like to add or discard things, or is it fine the way it is?

How do you feel about the theory that our surroundings reflect our inner state? Does a crowded work-space necessarily mean that our brain is 'cluttered'? Perhaps your brain is more like a back-pack than an orderly bookshelf. Think of it as overflowing with useful things which you can grab when you want them. If you are not happy with the contents of your workspace (or your back-pack) list those things again in order of priority and see whether you can discard some. Or do you need to acquire more? If the latter, read on. Otherwise skip the next two sections – you might be tempted.

Highly useful items

- Thesaurus.

- Dictionaries of proverbs and quotations.

- Rhyming dictionary.

- Current encyclopaedia for checking dates and information.

- Books of names.

- Hand-held cassette recorder for dictating as an alternative means of recording your words. (Try timed dictation as an alternative to timed writing.)

- For PC users, a voice-operated word processor as an alternative to the above.

- A large clock and a timer with an audible signal.

- Kettle, cup, tea, etc. – leaving the room to make drinks can be distracting.

- Answering machine and/or fax.

Treats

These are important. Here are a few suggestions.

- Aromatherapy oils in a burner or applied (suitably diluted) to the skin. Try: pine for inspiration, sage for opening to the subconscious, lavender, camomile and rose to relax, grapefruit to wake up, geranium to stimulate dreams.

- For a wonderful 'quick-fix', place a drop of oil on the centre of each palm, rub them together vigorously, then cup your hands over your nose and inhale deeply (many thanks to aromatherapist Ruth Wise for that idea).

- You might prefer to reward yourself with a large bar of chocolate, kept by a partner or friend and delivered at a specific time – with a cup of tea perhaps. Or a long soak in the bath might be more your style.

- How about a large comfy chair to snuggle into for hand-drafting or reading, with your favourite music close at hand?

Items for writing 'the right brain way'

The uses for these will be explained in subsequent chapters.

- tarot cards in your preferred style and tradition
- a collection of beautiful objects and pictures

- coloured pens and papers
- mirror
- magnifying glass, binoculars
- tape recorder
- small dictionary
- basic astrology text or programme (optional).

WRITING AND YOUR IDENTITY

Invent yourself as a writer

Your writing self may well express an aspect of your personality which is normally hidden from the world. Perhaps you have a high-powered job which requires you to be very 'left-brain', while your writing self is poetic and vulnerable. Or the reverse – you write horror, crime or erotic fiction and teach infants by day. Perhaps you write as a person of the opposite gender. If you write in a variety of genres, you may have several writing selves.

In order to manage any tension between these different facets of yourself, or to prevent one popping out at an inappropriate time, try 'fleshing them out', much as you would your fictional characters. Make them the subject of timed writing or a complete play or short story. Perhaps one of the functions of pen-names is to allow the writing self (or selves) and the everyday self to lead separate lives. In that case a writing self might benefit from the construction of his or her full autobiography.

Value yourself and your writing

How do you feel about writing as an occupation or pass-time? When you talk about it, do you feel proud – or embarrassed? Do you use the words ''only' or 'just' when you describe your work? Do you call it 'scribbling'? Do you think of writing as a worthy pursuit or, if you are a professional, as a 'proper' job? Do you feel justified in claiming time and space to do it? How do you feel about the writing you produce? Are you confident enough to submit it to publishers?

How do you cope with rejection letters? Have feelings about yourself as a writer affected your attitude to any of the suggestions in this chapter? For example, do you feel it is worth following the physical programme, setting up a workspace, claiming time, collecting a 'tool kit'? Are other things/other people 'more important?' Do you feel you are kidding yourself that you can do this?

It may be a while before you can give positive answers to these questions and really mean it – but, with perseverance it happens. An 'invented self' can be a huge help in this respect. A self that is feeling positive and strong can give the less confident one a pep-talk.

A supportive attitude from those close to you is also invaluable. A friend at the beginning of her writing career heard her husband tell a caller, 'My wife is a writer and cannot be disturbed.' She felt she could do anything after that.

$$\binom{2}{}$$

Tune In

As writers we need to fine-tune our senses to both our inner and our outer worlds. Whether we are observing people, objects, locations or situations, an important part of the process is paying close attention to what is happening *within ourselves* as we do so. Our inner experience of the world is what we communicate to others in our writing, so it is extremely important to be aware of ourselves and our feelings in relation to any aspect of the environment we wish to explore.

TO YOURSELF

The following exercises will help you to develop this vital skill. To gain the maximum benefit, they should be done in a completely relaxed state, with your eyes closed. As with all the visualisation exercises in this book, the instructions should be read onto a tape with sufficient pauses where necessary to allow the experience to unfold. Settle yourself somewhere comfortable where you will not be disturbed, before you play back the tape.

EXERCISE

Focus inwards

Become still. Let your breathing settle. Take your awareness inwards. What is your life like at this moment? As you consider this question, allow an image to emerge. Take your time. Let the image develop and reveal itself.

- What particular aspect of your life do you think this image represents? How do you feel about it?
- When you have finished exploring this image, draw it. Sit with it a while and get to know it even better. Give it a name.
- Would you like to change the image in any way? If so, make those changes.
- How do you feel about the image now?

Tune in physically

- Allow one hand to explore the other – slowly, carefully, as though it were an unfamiliar object. Notice the temperature, the texture, the different shapes.
- Which hand is doing the exploring? How does it feel in that exploring role?
- Transfer your attention now to the hand that is being explored. How does that feel? Focus on those feelings about being explored.
- Change the roles over. How does each hand feel now?
- If your right hand had a voice, what would it sound like? What would it say?
- Give your left hand a voice. What sort of voice is it? What does it say?
- Let your hands talk to each other for a while.
- Open your eyes. Record your experiences.

Did it feel strange to focus on yourself in that way? Some people find it makes them uneasy at first. They may even find themselves getting angry. ■

CASE STUDY

David, one of my more 'down-to-earth' students, had this reaction. He felt quite foolish about exploring his feelings and the first time he tried to write about himself with his left hand, he threw down the pen in frustration.

Other students have found the experience liberating. Sheila said she wished she had known earlier about this way of working.

Whatever your reaction to these tuning-in exercises, do persevere. Focusing on the self is an important habit for a writer to develop. Feelings about ourselves often influence our treatment of characters. See what links you notice in this respect after completing the next exercise.

Tune in to your self-image

Do this quickly, with as little thought as possible.

- Write the numbers 1–10 underneath each other 'shopping list' style.
- Beside each number write **one** word which describes you.
- Put this list aside and **forget it** by doing something else for ten minutes.

                    – 10 minute break –

- Now, on a fresh sheet of paper, write the numbers 1–10 again.
- With your **other hand** write ten words which describe you.
- Compare the two lists.

What did you discover in comparing lists? Were some words positive and some negative? Did you contradict yourself, even in the same list? Did the lists reflect different, perhaps contradictory, aspects of your personality?

Tune in to an internal dialogue

- Writing with each hand in turn, set up a dialogue about yourself.
- Ask questions about any aspects of your life that have been puzzling or annoying you. Let one hand ask and the other one answer. ■

Discover the critic within

Writing with the non-dominant hand, as we did in the last two exercises, puts us in the 'child place'. It can bring up feelings of vulnerability and frustration, making us impatient with ourselves. We may find ourselves thinking that exercises like this are just gimmicks or tricks which cannot produce anything 'truly creative'. Such reactions are often due to unhelpful messages we received about ourselves in childhood – messages which have stuck and which cause us to criticise ourselves today.

Once we recognise these 'old tapes' for what they are, we can learn to turn them off. 'No thank you.' 'What's *your* problem?' or simply 'Shut up!' are some of the more polite ways of dealing with these internal voices. Whose voices are they? If you can trace such messages to a specific individual or individuals, going back in your imagination and delivering the 'shut up' message personally can be a very liberating experience.

CASE STUDY

When David finally got in touch with his internal critic, he began to understand where his earlier feelings of frustration came from, and he decided to persevere with the exercises – for a while, at least.

Bypass the critic

The physical difficulty of writing with the non-dominant hand, distracts us from the words themselves. It is therefore a good way to bypass our internal critic. In doing this we free ourselves to rediscover the spontaneous creativity of childhood, and surprise ourselves with the results. Word association activities also enable us to bypass the critic, provided we allow ourselves to let go and write whatever comes into our heads. The two word-association exercises which follow, are useful tools at any stage in the writing process. In this case we will be using them as another way of tuning in to ourselves.

EXERCISE

Word Web

- ◆ In the centre of a clean sheet of A3 or A4 paper, write one word from the lists you made in the second exercise. Circle it.
- ◆ Radiating from this circle, draw six short 'spokes' (see Figure 2) and at the end of each spoke write a word you associate with the word in the centre.
- ◆ From each of these six words, quickly write a succession of associated words, continuing each spoke to the edge of the page.
- ◆ Now let your eye roam around the page. Soon words will begin to group themselves into unexpected phrases. For example; the 'energetic' person in (Figure 2) might come to life on the page as a *manic walker* with an *exercise mat* in their *back-pack*, a *forty* year old *battery hen* or even a *balloon* in *blue rompers*. Such phrases are unlikely to result from logical thinking processes.

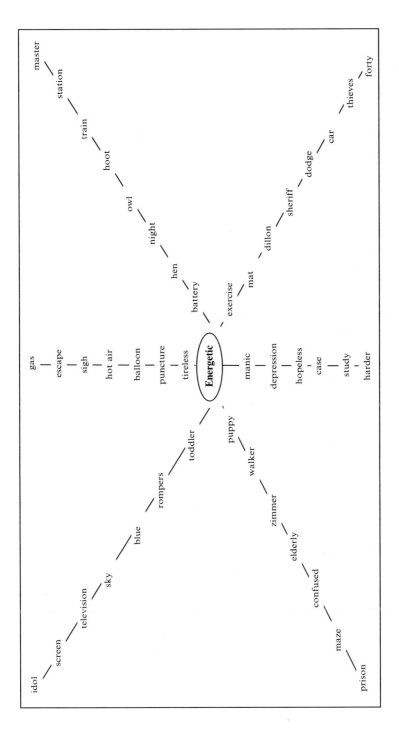

Fig. 2. Example of a word web.

Word Grid 1

- Divide a sheet of paper into three columns and label them 'DAY', 'MONTH' 'YEAR'.
- Divide the paper horizontally into 12 sections and number them 1–12.
- In each of the boxes you have created in the first column, write an adjective, chosen at random. In each of the second column boxes, write a random noun. In each of the third column boxes write a random verb – any tense. For example:

	DAY	MONTH	YEAR
1	bright	corner	cures
2	exuberant	schoolroom	corrupted
3	deep	ramp	charging
4	green	pudding	congeal
5	feckless	tiger	erupted
6	domineering	cupboard	swimming
7	uncaring	theatre	performs
8	reverential	attic	flickers
9	shameless	cauliflower	enfolding
10	solitary	army	slides
11	authoritarian	grandmother	march
12	world-weary	directions	collapses

- Choose a random date – yours or a friend's birthday, a historical date, your next dentist appointment – anything. Write it in number form e.g. 25/12/2004.

- The two digits of the day in the example given – 25 – add up to 7, so the adjective would be number 7 in the 'DAY' column – which is *uncaring*. The month is number 12, so the noun you have generated is *directions*. The digits of the year add up to 6, so the verb is *erupted*. This might generate the sentence 'His uncaring directions erupted into her consciousness', which you could tweak to suit your current needs, or put in your writer's notebook for another time. ■

Such word association exercises provide us with that wonderful idea-trigger *unexpected juxtaposition* which can take our writing along some very surprising routes.

CASE STUDY

Karen particularly liked grids and webs and would use them to generate several sentences at a time, which she would then use as the starting point for a poem. She often used grids in the same way as webs, by simply letting her eyes move around the collection of words until a phrase 'jumped out' and appealed to her.

A quick way of generating similarly unexpected three-word sequences is to open any book at random and choose the first adjective, the first noun and the first verb that meet your eye.

A word grid can be used in a different way, to generate a series of words which provide the theme of a story. This time only nouns are used.

EXERCISE

Word Grid 2

	DAY	MONTH	YEAR
1	lorry	sea	jackdaw
2	barn	fishmonger	school
3	woman	mountain	steam-roller
4	dinner	aircraft hangar	conductor

5	diamond	typewriter	knife
6	cat	detective	supermarket
7	murder	stress	vodka
8	soldier	biro	branch
9	astronaut	beans	cabinet
10	poison	joy	music
11	toaster	roof	crocodile
12	instructions	hair	medicine

Again, choose a random date – say 14/02/1939. This time the digits of the day add up to 5, so the first word is **diamond**. The month is 2, so the second word is **fishmonger** and the digits of the year add up to 22, which adds up to 4 – so the next word is **conductor**. Your story is therefore going to be about a **diamond**, a **fishmonger** and a **conductor**. ■

Word webs move outwards from a central idea. Word grids create an idea from a series of stimuli. The next technique takes the process full circle by moving inwards from a number of ideas towards a central focus.

EXERCISE

Word Honeycomb

- ◆ In the centre of an A3 or A4 sheet, circle a space for a word. Leave it empty.
- ◆ Choose sixteen words from the lists you made in the second exercise. Write eight along the top edge and the others along the bottom. (See Figure 3.)
- ◆ Starting with the top line, find a word which connects the first two words and write it below with two connecting lines, as shown. Find a word to connect words 3 and 4, 5 and 6, 7 and 8.

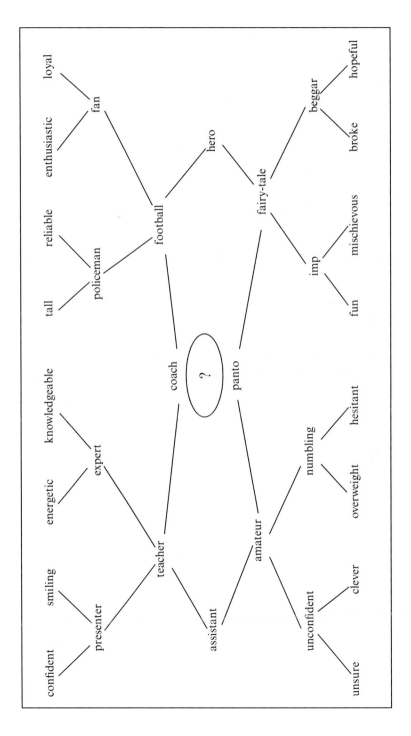

Fig. 3. A word honeycomb.

- ◆ From the new line formed, find a word to connect words 1 and 2, 3 and 4, positioning them below, as before.
- ◆ Find a connecting word for the two words in the new line, and write it above the space you have marked out.
- ◆ Repeat this process, working upwards from the bottom of the page.
- ◆ Taking the third line from the top and the third line from the bottom, find a word to connect the two words on the left (*teacher* and *amateur* in Figure 3) and another to connect the two words on the right (*football* and *fairytale*). Write them on either side of the marked space, as shown.
- ◆ Find a word or a person which connects all four central words, as shown.

In Figure 3, the words **coach** and **panto** suggest 'Cinderella'. This could lead to **Buttons** as the **assistant hero** in that story. The person using the grid could ask, 'How am I like Buttons? Am I a good friend? Do I sometimes keep a low profile – and am I happy with that? How am I not like Buttons at all?' ■

The characters we invent in our writing are products of our subconscious and reflect aspects of ourselves – whether we are aware of it or not. The way in which we react to people around us is influenced by the same subconscious processes and may say more about us than about them. If the characters in our stories are two dimensional or unconvincing, it could be because we are out of touch with these processes. The exercises in this book will help you to develop the awareness needed to engage with them. Such awareness is a vital tool for writers who are really serious about their work.

TO ANOTHER PERSON

This exercise can be used in supermarket queues, doctor's waiting-rooms, airport lounges or any other place where we find ourselves spending any length of time among strangers. You will need to make brief notes.

EXERCISE

◆ Choose a person to focus on and stand or sit near them.

◆ Note three things you know about them (straight observation).

◆ Note three things you feel about them (your 'gut reactions').

◆ Note three things you imagine about them.

These notes represent your reactions to the person in question at three different levels, from here and now 'reality' to pure fantasy, all of which originate in your subconscious. Even in 'straight observation', your choice of things to notice was influenced in this way. You now have nine attributes on which to base a fictional character.

You could add a few more notes at each level, do a short timed writing about your new character with these attributes in mind – or focus on a new person and give your fist character someone with whom to interact.■

This exercise can also be done in pairs with someone you know just a little. I often use it as one of the opening exercises when beginning work with a new group. This situation offers an opportunity for discussion and feedback, which can be very useful.

Students who spend a little time 'tuning in' before doing the third part of the exercise, have often reported that some of the things they imagined were pretty close to the truth.

USING THE TECHNIQUES YOU HAVE LEARNED

Active engagement with our subconscious processes enables us to know our characters intimately and therefore transfer them convincingly to the page.

CASE STUDIES

When Sheila managed to free some days for writing, she was surprised at how enjoyable it was and at how easily it flowed, using these methods. She then felt that her suspicions about putting it off in case she was unable to do it well enough were confirmed. She concluded that the BBC's decision not to perform her play probably affected her confidence more than she realised. Casting the producer in question as her 'inner critic' and conducting an inner dialogue with her, helped Sheila to move on. Using these techniques over a number of weeks helped her to rediscover playfulness and a sheer joy in writing that she had not felt for some time.

As for David, after getting some intriguing results from Word Webs and successfully using a Word Honeycomb to discover 'whodunit', he was very pleased that he had not given up. He admitted that he had identified a particularly scathing English teacher as one of the 'voices' of his inner critic and that this had motivated him to persevere 'and jolly well show him'!

Checklist

◆ What have you learned about yourself through doing these exercises?

◆ How will you use this in your writing?

◆ What have you learned about your internal critic?

◆ How will you deal with your critic in future?

◆ How will you use: word association, writing with the non-dominant hand?

TO YOUR CHARACTERS

Use what you know

EXERCISE

As suggested above, the first step to knowing your characters is knowing yourself. Ask 'how am I like/unlike this person? How do I feel about them? Who do they remind me of?' Write some of the answers with your non-dominant hand.

Next, choose one word to describe this character. Make it the centre of a web. Or use both hands to make two eight-word lists, then build a honeycomb. ■

Use your imagination

EXERCISES

a) To converse with your character

Tune in to this person's speech. How do they sound? What gestures do they use? What is their accent like?

◆ Imagine they are sitting opposite you, and talk to them.
◆ Write a dialogue between this character and a character which represents some aspect of yourself – your left-hand self maybe, or your internal critic. Is the speech of each character quite distinct, or is it sometimes unclear which one of you is speaking? How can you improve on this?

b) To do five-minute writings about your character

If this person were . . . an animal, flower, fruit, piece of music – what would it be? **If they found themselves** on a desert island, naked at a concert, having tea with the Queen, they would . . . **This person's deepest darkest secret is that they** . . . **When this person makes a cup of tea/mows the lawn they** . . . (Choose any everyday task, not necessarily appropriate to the character's period. Heathcliffe doing the weekly shop for example, could be quite revealing.)

c) To do 10 x 10

Make a grid, ten spaces down and ten across, big enough to write a few words in each space. Down the side of the grid list ten aspects of a character's life: clothes, musical tastes, favourite food, pet hates, etc. With the minimum of thought, fill in the grid by brainstorming ten facts about each of those aspects (see Figure 4).

You now have 100 facts about your character. Because you did not consider them carefully first, some of these things may seem quite off-the-wall. Good. These are probably the ones which will make the character live – the unexpected or secret things which makes him or her unique. You will not use all these facts when you write about the character – but you will *know* them. This will make the character feel more and more alive to you. ■

Discover more

EXERCISE

Left side/right side

Most people's faces reveal different personality traits on each

CLOTHES	Homemade	Too pretty	Old fashioned	Wants jeans	Hides DMs at Gran's	Hates bonnets	Holes in socks	Nurse's outfit	Two of everything	Matching knickers
MOODS	'Sweet'	Catty	Unpredictable	Fed up	Vulnerable	Stormy	Rebellious	Cooperative	Trusting	Devious
FOOD	Loves chocolate	Allergic to nuts	Hates tomatoes	Likes bread	Loves jam sandwiches	Apples are OK	Goes hyper on oranges	Swallows prune pits	Feeds cat spinach	Bakes own cakes
COLOURS	Favourite is blue	Hates red	Wants to wear black	Paints in pastels	Dyes hair purple	Likes stripes	Hates checks	Hates brown	Painted room pink	Has pink duvet
FRIENDS	Lucille Locket	Bridie O'Peep	M. Muffett (Spinster)	Call her 'Rosie'	Live some way away	Take advantage	Don't often visit	Gossip about her	She wants new ones	Has put ad in paper
PETS	Budgie	Goldfish	Snake	Tarantula	Keeps in bedroom	Allergic to fur	Would like a duck	Animals like her	Wants a pig	Hates poodles
MUSIC	Plays the piano	Can't sing	Wants a drum set	Likes Oasis	Mother likes Cliff	Hates opera	Likes heavy metal	Loves string quartets	Writes her songs	Dad plays concertina
HOBBIES	Reading Sci-Fi	Painting	Embroidery	Knitting	Listening to Radio 2	Planning robberies	Dying hair	Trying out make-up	Plays drums in a band	Wind-surfing
TALENTS	Good with animals	Good listener	Tastes good	Good cook	Good seamstress	Good with colours	Musical ability	Persuasive talker	Leadership potential	Criminal potential
FLAWS	Thinks she can sing	Over-confident	Gullible	Short-sighted	Vain	Quick temper	Abrasive	Untruthful	Eats too much	Secret drinker

Fig. 4. 10 x 10: Red Riding Hood.

side. This often represents the self they show the world and the more hidden self.

Ask a friend or partner to cover each half of their face in turn. Describe what you see each time. Compare the two descriptions. Were you surprised?

Repeat the exercise with any full-face photograph. Now place a mirror down the centre of the face to view the wholly left-sided/right-sided person.

Repeat the exercise with a full-face photograph of somebody who resembles your character. This is another way to make your characters multi-dimensional.

Guided visualisation

Tape these instructions and listen to them in a relaxed state with closed eyes. Speak slowly, leaving sufficient pauses for the experience to unfold. Switch the tape off and make notes at intervals to suit yourself.

Bring your character into your awareness. Visualise them in every detail. Notice their size, their shape, the way they stand or sit . . . About how old are they?

When you have a clear picture in your mind, try to hear the character's voice . . .

What sort of mood are they in? What is the first thing they might say to you?

What does this person smell like? Is it the smell of their house or workplace?

What is this person's house like? Is it clean and tidy, or in a muddle? Do they have any pets? What do the different parts of the house smell like? What can you hear as you move around this house?

Become your character for a while. Take on their mood . . .

Look down at the clothes you are wearing . . . How do they feel against your skin? Who chose these clothes? Are you happy in them?

How are you standing? How does it feel to walk around . . . to sit?

What can you see out of the windows? Are there any neighbours? How do you get on with the people living nearby? Who visits the house? Who do you visit?

What did you have for breakfast today? How did you eat it? What is your attitude to food in general?

How do you spend your time? How do you enjoy yourself – and when?

Add any other questions you need to ask.

Do you have a name for your character? If not, tune in again and ask them. Also ask how they feel about that name and who chose it.

How do you feel about the character now?■

Use tarot cards
Tarot cards represent powerful archetypal energies – the collective human experience underlying legend, myth and folklore. Many types and style of deck are available from book stores and 'New Age' shops, and through mail or Internet order. They should always be treated with great respect. Used with awareness, the tarot offers profound insight into our own lives and those of our characters.

EXERCISE

Separate from the rest of the pack the cards depicting people. From these, either select one which reminds you of your character, or place the cards face downwards before choosing, thus inviting fate to take a hand.

If you chose the card consciously, note your reasons for doing so. Then write down everything both observed and imagined about the character on the card. Use some of the techniques you have learned in this chapter to help you.

Note any surprises. Look at the card for a while. Let it 'speak' to you.

If you chose the card at random, consider it as an aspect of the character of which you were unaware. Work with it as above. Alternatively, choose from the whole pack, with the chance of considering your character as an animal, object or place – as in the timed writing above. Or choose a card to represent a new character entirely. ■

Many tarot sets come with a manual, and this will provide additional insight.

Use unexpected juxtaposition

Word webs jolt us out of our language rut by placing words in unusual groupings. Placing our characters in unaccustomed social or geographical settings has a similar effect (see *Heathcliffe getting the weekly shopping* above).

How would:

- ◆ Scarlett O'Hara control a class of infants?
- ◆ Gandalf organise the teas at a church garden fete?

◆ Jane Eyre relate to Romeo, or Robinson Crusoe to Ophelia?

EXERCISE

Write one of your characters into a scene from your favourite
novel. What can you learn about them from their reactions?
(For parents and teachers of teenagers: revitalise flagging
interest in a set book by the introduction of a favourite
media character, e.g. Lara Croft visits *Pride and Prejudice*.)

- ◆ Draw a tarot card at random and get your character to
  interact with the person, place or situation depicted. Pay
  particular attention to the dialogue.
- ◆ Choose a date at random and get your character to interact
  with each of the objects or qualities generated by that date
  your (nouns only) word grid. ■

Checklist
Bring your characters to life by:

- ◆ asking how they are like/unlike you, and exploring your feelings
  about them
- ◆ talking with them
- ◆ using word webs, honeycombs, timed writing and '10 x 10'.
- ◆ considering both sides of their face/character
- ◆ using guided visualisation
- ◆ using tarot cards
- ◆ putting the character in an unaccustomed setting or having
  them interact with an unexpected object or quality.

TO AN OBJECT

Focusing on an object usually indicates either its significance to
the plot, or its relationship to one of the characters. The

condition of an object may provide clues to a person's lifestyle or may be used as a metaphor for their mood.

Techniques for tuning into ourselves and into a character can also be used for tuning into an object. Also, ask who found it or made it, when and where. Invent a history for its finder/maker and imagine its journey from the point of origin to the point at which it arrived in your story.

Another very useful technique is to speak as the object, in the first person. 'I am a grubby white telephone – much used, pawed, put down, buttons pressed, never really seen by anyone . . .' and so on.

This will tell you things about your character or yourself, and may also start you off on a completely new story.

TO SETTINGS

Again, most of the techniques described so far can be used in relation to a setting. Speaking as the setting in the first person is particularly effective when landscape and weather are seen as reflective of a character's mood.

Use alternate hands to dialogue with the landscape. When you have a name for the place, use this as the centre of a web.

Tarot cards are also very useful, whether you work directly with a setting or choose another type of card to use as a metaphor.

EXERCISE

Timed writing

Think of a setting you have experienced which is similar to the one in your story. Begin 'I remember . . .' and write for ten minutes.

'I don't remember . . .' also brings up some interesting details.

Guided visualisation

Tape, as before. Listen in a relaxed state with closed eyes.

Find yourself in the location of your story. Really feel you are there . . .

What time of day is it? Are there people around? Animals? What is the weather like? What time of year is it? What historical period?

Start to explore . . . Look . . . Touch . . . Feel the air against your skin What can you hear? . . . Smell? Can you taste anything?

What is the atmosphere of this place? Do you feel comfortable here?

What is the pace like – lively? Slow? Is it in tune with your mood?

What is the name of this place? See it written on a sign saying 'Welcome to. . .'

Take another walk around. Find a door or a road or pathway that you have not noticed before. Where does it lead you?■

TO A SITUATION

The Mythic and the Osho Zen tarot decks vividly depict a variety of situations. Work with them as you did with characters and settings. Describe what you see, record your feelings (writing with both hands if appropriate) let the card 'speak'. Use webs, honeycombs, and timed writing. Consult the manuals for further insight. Many newspaper photographs also capture the essence of the moment and are a very good resource for tuning in, using the techniques described.

Create tension and mystery

EXERCISES

Work outdoors

Use binoculars. Imagine you are watching a film. Survey the territory, then suddenly focus on one feature. Imagine the soundtrack playing a couple of loud chords. The feature immediately assumes huge significance and your imagination turns a somersault.

Work with a picture

Use a magnifying glass and a printed picture with a reasonable amount of detail (e.g. a photograph, postcard, picture from a magazine or holiday brochure).

Let your eye roam over the picture, then suddenly magnify – a car – an open window – a clock on a steeple – a group of people. Each time, imagine an appropriately attention grabbing soundtrack. What could it mean?

- Make one of these magnified features the subject of a five-minute timed writing. ■

Checklist

New techniques:

♦ speak as an object or setting, in the first person
♦ use a magnifying glass or binoculars.

CASE STUDY

The techniques described in this chapter can be very powerful and can greatly enhance your writing. However, they cannot be rushed and for students like Karen, who can only find short periods of time in which to write, this can be a problem. Karen found she could use her snatched moments in the car for timed writing and word webs, but not for tuning in or any kind of guided visualisation. Eventually she cleared one weekly slot when the children were in bed, unplugged the phone and put a 'do not disturb' notice on the front door. She let friends and family know that she would not be available at that time. Like the 'ten minutes a day' commitment, while not ideal, it is another way of working around a current life-situation which does not leave much room for writing. Karen feels it also has a positive side in bringing discipline and focus to her work.

Discover the Plot

The average plot is constructed around three basic elements:

1. Conflict. Something happens to disturb the status quo.

2. Character response and evolution – the character may be strengthened in their resolve, or they may change.

3. Resolution of conflict.

Sometimes we begin with a very clear idea of 1 and/or 3, but only a hazy idea about our characters and their environment. Sometimes the reverse happens – a character or a place grabs our attention then gradually begins to tell us their story. Whatever our starting point – plot or character, the narrative process should gradually unfold as a complex interaction between the two. Plot cannot work where its demands go against the nature of the characters. Characters become uninteresting and lose their authenticity if tailored to fit the demands of the plot. Both storyline and characters can seem to assume a life of their own at times, suddenly taking unexpected turns 'all by themselves'.

Once we are aware of these processes we can make them work for us, so that we can follow a plot as it develops, rather than struggle to think what should happen next.

WHOSE STORY IS IT ANYWAY?

When characters and/or setting are vague we can get to know them better by using various ways of 'tuning in'. When characters and/or setting develop first, they can help us to discover the plot. The following guided visualisations help to enhance character–plot interaction. They can be used to develop a new plot, or to work on a current one.

Tape all three sets of instructions first with appropriate pauses (as in Chapter 2).

◆ If this is new work, choose a character from your tarot pack, writer's notebook, or your surroundings, and spend some time tuning in to them.

◆ If you wish to work on a current project, let one of the main characters come into your mind. Take some time to reacquaint yourself fully with this character before proceeding to the exercise.

◆ Have your writing materials near to hand *or*

◆ Respond aloud to the questions. Record the whole journey, including your responses, on a second tape-recorder.

EXERCISES

Guided visualisation (1)

Bring your character fully into your awareness now. What mood is their face and their posture expressing? Ask them what has happened to them today. Where have they been? Who have they met?

Was it an unusual, or an average day? How has it left them feeling?

Become this person now. Step into their skin, their clothing. Begin to move as they move, and speak as they speak. What can you see around you? What can you hear, feel, smell, taste? Notice the qualities of the light, the temperature and humidity. How does it feel to be in that place?

Find somewhere to sit quietly and reflect on your day and the events which led up to it. Gradually let your mind move backwards over your life, so that the events leading up to what happened here, today in this place become clear to you. Notice your feelings as you do this.

How do you see today in terms of your life as a whole? What do you think might happen next? How are you feeling now?

When you are ready, open your eyes.

◆ Write as your character in the first person. Make these experiences the subject of a ten-minute timed writing. Begin 'My life has been . . . '

Guided visualisation (2)

When you are ready, close your eyes and return to the place where you met your character.

Your character is not here. Spend some time exploring on your own.

Someone is approaching. You can see them nearby. They want to make contact. This person likes to gossip. They are eager to tell you their version of the events which your character described earlier. Listen to what they have to say. Ask any questions you want to ask, but do not argue.

When you are ready, draw this conversation to a close, take your leave of the gossiping person, and open your eyes.

♦ As the gossip, in the first person, write your version of the events you have just described. Record your feelings as you write. When you are ready, close your eyes and return to that place.

Guided visualisation (3)

Almost immediately a person approaches. They are anxious to talk with you. It becomes clear that this is a person in whom your character has confided. They can be trusted. They have news of what is happening to your character now. Listen carefully. Ask whether your character needs your help in any way. The trusted friend wants to put the record straight about what the gossip told you. Discuss this for a while. Make sure you now have the correct information. When you are ready, draw this conversation to a close, thank the trusted friend, take your leave of them and open your eyes.

♦ So what is the 'real' story? Write a dialogue between the gossip and the trusted friend. Use two different coloured pens. Try writing with both hands.

Outline the plot

Write a brief resume of the story so far. What overall theme is developing? Choose at the most **three** words to describe the key theme(s) of your story. Imagine a snappy description on a book-jacket: '**This is a story of** – – – , – – – **and** – – – '

Here are some suggestions:

adventure	anarchy	avarice	betrayal
bitterness	brutality	chaos	confusion
constancy	courage	devotion	disintegration
discovery	disempowerment	disgust	enmity

envy	escape	fanaticism	fear
friendship	frustration	greed	growth
gullibility	hardship	hatred	hedonism
inequality	innocence	integrity	intimidation
intolerance	jealousy	justice	loss
love	mayhem	mystery	obsession
opposition	power	pride	punishment
purpose	pursuit	rebellion	recovery
release	rescue	revenge	sacrifice
sacrilege	search	secrets	selfishness
shame	temptation	transformation	trickery
victory	vulnerability	wisdom	youth

Precisely identifying the theme(s) in this way keeps your writing focused. This is particularly important when writing a short story. Keep returning to the theme and checking it out: 'This is a story about x, y and z – am I making this clear? Am I reinforcing this theme, or am I losing the impact by getting side-tracked?' In a longer narrative, staying focused on the main theme is important for developing sub-plots which enhance rather than distract from the main action. ■

Checklist

♦ Let your character tell their story and their feelings about it.

♦ Let other characters tell you their version.

♦ Briefly outline the story as you see it.

♦ Identify the key theme(s).

♦ Keep returning to the key themes and checking them out.

EXERCISES

If you are stuck for ideas, try using the list of words above as a starting point.

- Pick two or three words at random and take them as the basic themes for your story.
- Use random words from the list to complete the sentence 'This is a story about – – – , – – – and – – –'. Make it the beginning of a piece of timed writing.

You could also make a **plot grid**, similar to the ideas grids we looked at in the previous chapter. This time, divide your page into four columns and label them: CHARACTER, SETTING, CATALYST, MOTIVE. Draw ten horizontal lines and number them 0–9. Proceed as follows:

- Choose – or ask a friend to choose – ten single-word identity descriptions e.g. plumber, brunette, husband, gossip, and write them in the CHARACTER column.
- Choose ten locations – some large some small scale e.g. Rome, Westminster Abbey, dentist's waiting room – and write them in the SETTINGS column.
- Choose ten objects, events or persons which are likely provoke action or reaction of some sort – e.g. lost umbrella, nun, unexploded bomb – and write them in the CATALYST column.
- Finally, choose ten 'motivating factors' – e.g. ambition, jealousy, greed – and list them in the MOTIVE COLUMN.

For example:

	Character	**Setting**	**Catalyst**	**Motive**
0	spy	hotel	power cut	desperation
1	sales rep	the vets	balloon bursts	envy
2	blonde	county court	new car	power

3 actress	back yard	war	self-hate
4 bully	Berlin	a death	love
5 darts player	cathedral	bath time	ambition
6 gardener	kitchen	illness	greed
7 prince	launderette	lost jacket	revenge
8 nurse	tunnel	birthday	pride
9 judge	runway	puppy	humour

Now choose a random 4-digit number. This could be a pin-number, the year of your birth or any other historical event, or any combination you choose. Use this number as you used the dates in the previous chapter, to provide you with a skeleton plot. For example, the year 1066 would give you a **sales rep** in an **hotel** with an **illness** and motivated by **greed.** ■

INVENT AN AUDIENCE

As soon as all these preparations are complete and the real story telling begins, we need an audience; initially one specific person to whom we can convey our thoughts. Without this externalised third party, our writing can become a private conversation with our characters. Our reader may feel like a late arrival at a party, bewildered and excluded. Increasing introspection can also cause us to lose sight of our ideas – as if they have disappeared into a black hole. This particular manifestation of so-called 'writer's block' can be reversed by focusing our thoughts outwards again.

♦ Take a few minutes to write about a recent event in your life.

♦ Now write 'Dear . . .' and describe the same event in a letter to a friend.

♦ What differences did you notice?

Who would you like to be the recipient of your story? Will it be someone you know, or someone you invent? What do you need from them?

If your story is intended for a specific market, say a particular women's magazine, visualise one representative of that audience. Use a guided journey, left-hand writing, webs, 10x10, etc. to become fully acquainted with this person, then deliver your story just to them.

If your priority at this stage is to tell your story clearly, invent (or remember) your listener as one of those irritating people who asks a question after every few sentences.

CASE STUDY

David decided to conjure up his ex-boss, who was an absolute perfectionist. Nothing got past him it seemed. David had found this very irritating at the time, but – as with the discouraging English teacher – admitted he was motivated to do his best 'just to show him'. Imagining his boss as his audience helped him to achieve similar standards in his writing. It also helped him to sustain the 'nit-picking' attention to detail necessary for writing good crime fiction.

If style and quality are your main concern, invent someone who is not easily satisfied, who expects the best from you and wants you to get it just right. Remember – whoever you choose, they are there for your benefit. Select the audience which you will find most stimulating and enabling – or the one which is most challenging, if that is what you feel you need.

◆ Try different listeners at different stages in the story's development.

- ◆ Invite your listener to contribute to the story.

- ◆ Tarot cards, family photographs, china ducks, your pets – anything, can be your audience.

- ◆ Switch roles and *be* the audience. Have your say from this seat too.

CASE STUDY

After Karen had been writing for several months in the privacy of her car, she began to feel her poetry was becoming too introspective. She thought that other people might not understand it. While discussing this with the writing group, she remembered that when she wrote as a teenager – even in her diary – she imagined she was talking to someone of her own age. She had recently bought the Arthurian Tarot, and felt particularly drawn to the Grail Maiden. She found it easy to imagine her as a receptive audience, and this helped her to direct her work outwards again.

Checklist

Inventing an audience enables you to:

- ◆ focus
- ◆ direct your ideas outwards
- ◆ consider your readers' needs
- ◆ tell your story clearly
- ◆ gain a new perspective.

PLAY ALL THE PARTS

Swiss psychoanalyst and mystic, Carl Jung suggests that everything we dream represents an aspect of ourselves. If we dream we are having tea with a cat in a pink swimsuit, we are the cat, the swimsuit, the tea itself, the place where the tea is served and so on. When we work with a dream, insight can be obtained by communicating with or becoming each of the parts in turn (see Chapter 7 for further information). Communicating with or through all aspects of our visualisations, gives us insight and also many new viewpoints to work with. Either tape your responses to the following exercise, or make them the subject of timed writing.

EXERCISE

- ◆ Return to the first visualisation in this chapter and find yourself in the place where you met your character. Notice the things around you. Talk with them.
- ◆ Speak as each of the objects in turn now. Speak as the character's clothing and footwear. Tell the story from each of these points of view.
- ◆ Speak as the place. Talk about all the things you have observed. ■

Checklist
Playing all the parts enables us to:

- ◆ get the most out of our visualisations
- ◆ gain new insight and new perspectives.

LET FATE TAKE A HAND
Games of chance
Introducing an element of chance, injects new life into our characters, our plot – and us.

Scrabble
1. Play a 15-minute game, either by yourself or with a friend. At the end of that time, write a story using every word you have made.

2. Or instead of recording the scores, record each word. Use them in the order in which they appeared.

3. Alternatively, use only the nouns or only the verbs which appeared. Make each the focus of a stage in your plot. Suppose the verbs you made were:

   plan   pack   doubt   arrange   saw   spend

A sample plot outline could read:

◆ Emily **plan**s to surprise her husband Tim with a party on their anniversary.

◆ She tells him to keep that day free. 'I **doubt** I shall be here,' he says.

◆ He starts to **spend** a lot of time away from home and seems preoccupied.

◆ A friend tells Emily that she **saw** Tim coming out of a hotel with his secretary.

◆ Devastated, Emily cancels the party and **pack**s her case to leave.

◆ Tim has been planning to celebrate their anniversary with a second honeymoon. His secretary has been helping him to **arrange** it.

Boggle, Lexicon, Jitters and other word games – such as *Target Words*, found in various newspapers and magazines – can be used in the same way.

Snakes and Ladders
Throw the dice and move a counter accordingly. Whatever number you land on, take a dictionary or choose a book at random and

open it at that page. Close your eyes and point to a word. Use it in your opening sentence. Continue in this way for each sentence. If you go up a ladder, let something positive occur in your character's life. If you go down a snake, introduce an obstacle or misfortune. The story ends after a set number of throws, or when you reach the last square.

◆ If you have a Monopoly set, use the 'Chance' and 'Community Chest' cards when you encounter a ladder or a snake.

◆ Draw a tarot card if you land on a snake, a ladder or any number divisible by five (or other number of your choice).

Any dice and counter board game can be adapted in this way. Or you can invent your own board game to suit your plot production needs.

Dice

1. Use a pair of dice and a dictionary. Devise your own word finding rules. For example, the first throw gives you a page number, the second tells you where it comes on that page (1st, 2nd, etc.) Or choose a word at random and throw the dice count forward that number of words and use the word you land on. Throw again to find the next word and so on. Use the words as in the games described above.

2. Use a single die and tarot cards. Shuffle the cards and select 30 unseen. Deal face down into six adjacent piles of five. Throw the die. The number thrown indicates the number of the pile from which to choose the first card. Throw and choose six times. Each card reveals the next stage of the plot.

3. Dice are traditionally used for divination and insight. The meanings attributed to their scores can also be used in story-making (see next section).

Checklist
Use games of chance:

◆ to write a whole story
◆ to give your plot an unexpected twist
◆ to reveal new aspects of your characters
◆ when you are stuck.

CASE STUDY

David found playing Scrabble and throwing dice extremely useful for discovering the next part of a story, or for creating really unexpected plot twists. Leaving the plot to chance seemed strange at first, but now he is hooked and regularly uses games of chance alongside more conventional approaches. Karen found these methods excellent for writing poetry. She would usually set herself a task, such as writing down the words in order and using each one to begin or end a line, or using them anywhere in the poem as long as they appeared in order. She would then see where this took her and use her artistic judgement to deviate from her self-imposed rules if she felt this would improve the work.

Predictive and 'inner wisdom' techniques
The techniques described are ancient systems for attuning ourselves to archetypal energies and experiences, hence the term 'inner wisdom'. They are used for divination, personal insight and guidance and – as I have already said – must be treated with care and respect. Approached in this way, they can also give insight into our characters and their stories.

Tarot spreads

The patterns in which the cards are laid are known as *spreads*. Many different spreads are described in the books and leaflets which accompany tarot packs. We can use these spreads to ask questions about our own lives and about the lives of our characters. The answers can also be read as an unfolding story. 'The Flying Bird' spread (Figure 5) works particularly well with the Osho Zen Tarot, which depicts concepts rather than characters. A recent Flying Bird spread read:

1. *Here and Now*: Turning inwards
2. *Resistance/fear*: Participation
3. *Response to the fear*: Stress
4. *Inner support*: Healing
5. *External support*: Innocence
6. *Relaxation/acceptance*: Experiencing
7. *New awareness*: Inner voice

It gave rise to this story outline:

A woman in her forties has always wanted to dance (1) but is afraid of making a fool of herself (2). She finally psychs herself up to join a dance class, but when she gets there she feels unable to go in (3). A little girl (5) watching at the door tells her she longs to be in there dancing. The woman remembers feeling like that when she was young, and this gives here the courage she needs (4). Dancing at last, she feels positively euphoric (6).

Later she tells the tutor how hard it was for her to take that first step. The tutor says 'I know – I saw you talking to yourself out there' (7).

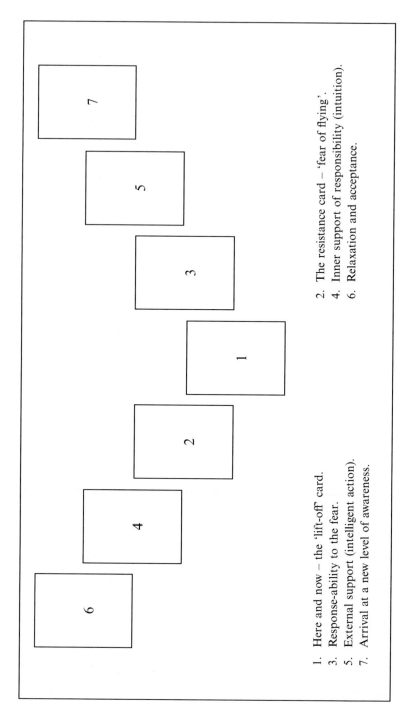

Fig. 5. Flying Bird tarot spread.

1. Here and now – the 'lift-off' card.
2. The resistance card – 'fear of flying'.
3. Response-ability to the fear.
4. Inner support of responsibility (intuition).
5. External support (intelligent action).
6. Relaxation and acceptance.
7. Arrival at a new level of awareness.

The I Ching

This ancient Chinese system involves asking a question, throwing three coins six times to obtain a hexagram, and interpreting this by consulting the I Ching – or *Book of Changes* (available in numerous editions, translations and interpretations). The answers are rich in metaphor. For example, from Hexagram 59 HUAN: *Clear what is blocking the light. Call a glass of water a pond if you like, but do not drown in it* or from Hexagram 64 WEI CHI: *A decisive new move but not if you behave like the centipede who, looking at his moving feet and analysing their order of movement, ends up on his back waving his thousand legs in the air.* The most useful answers result from sincere and well-formed questions. The answer to such questions, can reveal new aspects of a character, or change the plot dramatically. Many of the hexagrams offer a whole plot in themselves.

Runes

Norse in origin, each rune-stone bears an ancient alphabetical symbol. Bought sets include an accompanying booklet which gives the meaning of these. There are also many books on the subject available separately. Stones can be used singly or in spreads. As with the I Ching, answers can be interpreted in many ways. (The word *riddle – raedel* in Old English, comes from the Germanic *raedan* or 'reading'.) Some examples of runic food for thought are: from 1 THE SELF: *Not a time to focus on results look inside for the enemy of your progress* and from 5 TERMINATION/ NEW BEGINNINGS: *In deep water become a diver.*

Dice

Dice, traditionally three, can also be used as tools of divination and inner wisdom. There are many systems, some very complicated. For use in creating plots it is enough to know the basic meaning traditionally attributed to each score. These are:

3. A wish unexpectedly fulfilled.

4. Disappointment.

5. A stranger brings joy.

6. Loss – may bring spiritual gain.

7. Gossip causes unhappiness.

8. Ill-considered action may cause injustice.

9. Success, forgiveness, reunion.

10. Domestic contentment. Promotion.

11. Someone is ill.

12. A letter demands an answer.

13. Long-term sorrow.

14. A stranger becomes a close friend.

15. Temptation to make unjust deal.

16. A pleasant and profitable journey.

17. Foreigner gives good advice.

18. Excellent omen – promotion, profit, joy.

Dominoes

To help carry your plot forward, draw up to three dominoes (tradition says that more makes the dominoes tired!) Meanings are given as follows:

6/6: All round success. 6/5: Good works. 6/4: Litigation.

6/3: Short profitable voyage. 6/2: A useful gift. 6/1: Ending of an old trouble.

6/0: Be alert to treachery. 5/5: A good move. 5/4: Profit. Avoid speculation.

5/3: A helpful visitor. 5/2: Child-birth. 5/1: New love, sad ending.

5/0: Comfort a friend. 4/4: Stranger's party. 4/3: Disappointment. Courage.

4/2: A swindler is about. 4/1: Debts to be paid. 4/0: Attempt reconciliation.

3/3: A rival in love. 3/2: Do not tempt fate. 3/1: Surprising and useful news.

3/0: Jealousy causes trouble.

2/0: New relationship. Joy.

0/0: Bad omen. Loss, unhappiness.

2/2: Happy marriage.

1/1: Act now.

2/1: Loss of money or property.

1/0: Useful visit from stranger.

Checklist

Inner wisdom techniques:

◆ put us in touch with what we know deep down
◆ enable us to understand ourselves and our character
◆ supply interesting plots
◆ offer new perspectives.

There are also workbooks and computer programs for generating plots. Tom Sawyer and A.D. Weingarten's *Plots Unlimited* comes in both versions, and there is now an upgraded version of the software called *Storybase*. (See *Useful addresses and websites*.)

◆ Mix and match all these approaches.

WORK WITH ASTROLOGY

This is a brief introduction to a highly complex and comprehensive system, which bears little relationship to the familiar sun-sign 'horoscopes' found in the newspapers. These deal in an abridged and generalised way with just one aspect of our birth-chart – the sign the Sun was in when we were born. The word *horoscope* means 'map of the hour'. Our horoscope, or birth chart, shows the exact position of each planet at the moment of our birth, and is as unique as our finger-print. The science of Astrology has been painstakingly researched and refined over thousands of years. It charts the movements of ten planets, through twelve signs and twelve houses. It looks at the relationships of the planets to each other and to the system. It looks at the positions of planets now, in relation to their positions at the time we were born.

Each planet is associated with the characteristics of the deity after which it is named. For example, Neptune is seen as dreamy, creative and sometimes confused. Each Zodiac sign is also associated with one of the four elements (Earth, Fire, Air, Water) and demonstrates the qualities of that element. Each sign also has its own distinctive qualities. These factors 'colour' the attributes of planets found in the sign, for example, warlike Mars in fiery Aries might behave aggressively, whereas Mars in dreamy Pisces might have trouble making its presence felt. Poetic Neptune might feel 'like a fish out of water' in practical Capricorn.

The planets could be seen as actors on a stage and the signs as costumes, some of which fit well, and some quite the opposite. Planetary energies are also affected by their position in relation to each other and to areas of Cardinal, Fixed and Mutable energy. Then there are twelve Houses, representing the various stages of our journey through life and the way we interact with our environment. To borrow a phrase from psychology, the signs could be said to represent 'nature' and the houses 'nurture'. The appearance of planets in particular houses may either help or hinder our passage at that point.

Whatever our opinions regarding the validity of astrology, there is no doubt that it is a marvellous tool for writers. Once the basic principles are understood, we have only to choose a time, date and location for our character's birth – and endless possibilities for their development are revealed to us. Nowadays we do not even have to face the laborious task of drawing up a chart, as there are numerous software packages which will do it for us (see *Useful addresses*).

There are also specialised branches of astrology geared to specific purposes. Of particular interest to writers are:

1. *Age-point astrology* used by the Huber school (see *Useful addresses*) to chart significant periods in an individual's life.

2. *Horary astrology* which answers questions by drawing up a chart for the moment when the question was posed (great for crime writers).

3. *Synastry* which compares the chart of two individuals to discover the strengths and weaknesses of their relationship.

4. *Decumbiture* which was used hundreds of years ago by physicians and herbalists as a guide to prescribing remedies (useful for historical novelists).

5. *Astrocartography* advises on a choice of location, and the experiences we might have there at certain times.

CASE STUDY

Sheila has always been interested in astrology, and was intrigued by the idea of using it as a writing tool. She bought some astrological software, and found it so effective in helping to create rounded characters, that she may enrol in a correspondence course. She will assess how much time this would need, as she does not want to fall into her old pattern of distracting herself from writing.

Checklist

Astrology is an excellent tool for writers. Among other things it
helps us to:

◆ know our characters thoroughly

◆ plot the course of a character's life

◆ answer questions on any aspect which puzzles us

◆ see how two characters might relate

◆ decide the best location for our story.

All 'inner wisdom' techniques, including Astrology, work in
conjunction with our own energies. Your birth-chart, your dreams,
your reactions to words, images, people, places, situations are just
that – *yours*. A good astrologer, like a good dream worker or
good Tarot consultant, will not 'tell you what it means'.

He or she will explore the territory with you and facilitate your
discovery of what it means to *you*. A similar journey of discovery
is involved when using these techniques to enhance your writing.
Some of my students have been concerned that the use of such
methods is somehow 'cheating'. Not so – the wisdom is yours, the
journey is yours, the work is yours. In this chapter you have been
considering some of the ways in which you can access and make
use of your own creative power.

Using these methods, we are reminded that our 'inner workings'
are reflected in the outside world when we find ourselves drawing
the same cards, numbers and symbols again and again during
certain periods of our lives, or while engaged with a certain
character. Some we might never draw, while a friend seems to

draw them constantly. Deep inside we know the answers. These systems act as powerful tools, enabling us to contact that place of knowing for ourselves, for our characters and ultimately – if that is our intention – for our readers.

4

Develop Atmosphere, Pace and Mood

A good beginning grabs us, a skilful description engages our senses, a cleverly woven plot starts to intrigue us, we are warming to the characters, and then – we realise we have 'read' a couple of pages without taking in anything. Think of some books you found all too easy to put aside – that gathered dust beside the bed as you told yourself, 'I really must finish that.' What was missing?

Can you think of one that has recently satisfied most of the criteria at the beginning of this chapter, yet still failed to sustain your interest? Find it (if you have not thrown it away in frustration). Look at the first few chapters again. Having reacquainted yourself with it, how would you rate it in terms of:

- **atmosphere** – the 'something in the air' that intrigues, excites, seduces, unsettles – 'draws you in'.

- **pace** – is it crawling, cruising or speeding? Does it vary, or is it like a car with a stuck accelerator? Has the car broken down altogether?

- **mood** – in a sense, the 'inside-out' of atmosphere. Atmosphere affects a person's mood, and vice versa. How well does the author convey this?

If the author has got these right, you should feel 'part of the action'. You would probably have had some physical reactions, however subtle; prickles of uneasiness at the back of the neck, excited flutters in the chest, stirrings in the gut, an 'oh *no*' somewhere in the throat. Chances are, this was what was missing when you gave up on the book in question.

Now choose a book that really got to you – one that had you propping up your eye-lids at 3 a.m. because you just *had* to know what happened. Rate it on the same three aspects. How does it compare? Think of a film or TV drama that you would rate highly in this respect. Which were the memorable scenes? What was it that made those scenes so memorable? Do you notice any particular physical reactions as you recall them? Think of a TV advertisement or a piece of 'on-the-spot' newspaper reporting which you would also rate highly in this way. How was this impact achieved?

We can benefit greatly from studying the way these three elements are handled in a medium other than that for which we are writing. Videos/DVDs of successful screen dramas are particularly useful for this purpose – even more so if you can obtain the script (see *Useful addresses*).

Checklist
Skilful handling of atmosphere, pace and mood:

◆ draws you in
◆ makes you feel part of the action
◆ may be experienced physically
◆ is essential to a good read
◆ can be studied in a variety of media.

Choose a favourite video and novel to use as references as we work with each of these elements in turn.

CREATE AN ATMOSPHERE

A party with a really good atmosphere can 'take you out of yourself'. A party with no atmosphere has you casting surreptitious glances at your watch, wondering how soon is too soon to leave. It is the same with a story or a book. How do we create an atmosphere that makes people want to stay?

Find out how other writers do it

When writers are successful in creating atmosphere, they have probably immersed themselves in the setting (as discussed in Chapter 1). This is the first step. The following exercises help you to look at how experienced writers craft the material generated in this way.

- What sort of atmosphere is created in the opening pages of your chosen book? Is it a general 'feel' for the setting, or does it evoke a specific response?

- What words, phrases and images does the author use to achieve this?

- What are the main vehicles the author uses for this purpose, e.g. colour, sound, other sense impressions, action, contrasts, character's response?

- Use these as headings to sort the author's words in note form. 'Chunk' the sections on the page (see Chapter 1, Figure 1). This gives a clear overall picture, which offers considerable insight into the author's craft. It also makes the elements of that craft readily accessible as a stimulus for our own creativity.

◆ Repeat the exercise with some other favourite books.

◆ Repeat it with a favourite screen-drama video.

Use what you have learned

◆ Choose one page of notes from the previous section. Let your eye move at random around the chunks of words, until a particular phrase comes to the fore. Use it as the centre of a word web (see Chapter 2, Figure 2).

◆ Let your eye move around the word web until a new phrase emerges. Create atmosphere through 10 minutes of timed writing starting with this phrase.

◆ In **one** word describe the atmosphere you created.

◆ Write a word that means the opposite.

◆ Brainstorm everything that comes to mind when you say that word.

◆ Sort and chunk your words as above.

◆ Use these notes to write a piece evoking this opposite atmosphere.

◆ Choose one of the pieces you have written. Tape yourself reading it. Use this as a guided visualisation to stimulate ideas.

More ways of working

Let the surroundings create the atmosphere

As in the previous chapter, let the surroundings tell their story. If the place we were in could speak, what would its voice be like? What would it say? Choose a tarot card which evokes the same atmosphere as you want to create. Let it represent your setting. Let it speak.

Imagine a soundtrack

What sort of music would go with this place? Close your eyes and imagine a soundtrack accompanying your opening scenes. Let your inner camera move around the location, focusing on different features and bringing some of them into close-up. Let the soundtrack change and intensify as this occurs. If you have a suitable piece of music, play it as you read your work aloud.

CASE STUDY

Sheila worked outdoors with binoculars to help her create an atmosphere of tension and mystery (see Chapter 2). She also found it useful to take photographs to view through a magnifying glass at home and recreate that atmosphere. When she added an imaginary soundtrack to these techniques, she said she felt her writing come alive, giving it the 'edge' it was lacking. This made her more confident about continuing with the new play she had started to write for radio.

Work with a colour

For example, imagine something you own – or something connected with you in some way which is *red*. Allow it to become really vivid in your imagination. Make it *brighter*. Make it *bigger*. Imagine some stirring music to accompany this image. Make it *louder*. Imagine yourself in a crowd, wearing red, dancing around the object to this music in brilliant sunshine.

CASE STUDY

This approach really appealed to Zubin, one of my writing students who teaches art. He decided to incorporate painting into this exercise, and said he would discuss the results with the group the following week.

Play themed Scrabble

Sample themes: gothic, erotic, depressed, elated, Scandinavian, Mediaeval, Monday morning, Christmas, airport, garden fete. Only words which evoke the atmosphere in question are allowed. Use them as suggested in Chapter 3.

CASE STUDY

David found this a good way of generating sinister and threatening words as well as helping him gather a list of words to evoke the atmosphere of a police station. Karen found it a good way of combining family time with writing time. When she and another student, Shamina, got together with their children to play themed Scrabble, they came up with the idea in the next section.

Word Banks

CASE STUDIES

Like themed Scrabble, Karen and Shamina's Word Banks, help — among other things — to evoke atmosphere. They got the idea from one of the literacy activities at their children's primary school, where each pupil keeps a personal book for recording words they need to help them write. They decided to start their own books to record the words that came up in themed Scrabble.

After a while they felt that the nouns were not all that useful, whereas having a collection of verbs and adjectives to call on gave their writing a boost. Eventually they decided to move away from themed Scrabble and collect verbs and adjectives from anywhere and at any time that they presented themselves. They found that advertisements provided some particularly lively and unusual examples. Within a few weeks they had quite a large bank of words which they could dip into to give their writing extra interest.

Other students took the idea on board and came up with some suggestions for using these word banks. One was to simply let the eye roam around the page until something clicked (as we did with Word Webs in Chapter 2). Another way was to open the word bank book, point at random to a word and use it – unless it made absolutely no sense. Two examples I particularly remember from doing this with verbs were: (from David, describing a military academy) 'The windows **marched** across the front of the building' and (a fellow tutor, Pete, describing the sounds on a farm) 'The piglets were crackling in the straw' – a rather neat double meaning. David's example came from organising his word book into themes, so that he had brainstormed every verb he could think of to do with the army. Pete, being a great fan of unexpected juxtaposition, had collected his words at random, opened his book and pointed at random – and the foregoing was the happy result bestowed on him by fate.

Sheila organised her Word Bank alphabetically and, in some of her early drafts, experimented with replacing adjectives or verbs which she found uninspiring with others from her word bank beginning with the same letter. Children who previously **ran** into the play area now *ricocheted*, while the elderly gentleman who had **stepped gingerly** through them, now *slalomed gamely* – a much more lively and memorable image.

Checklist

To develop a sense of atmosphere:

- immerse yourself in the setting of your story
- study the work of other writers
- let the surroundings speak
- imagine a sound track
- work with a colour
- play themed Scrabble

♦ build up a Word Bank to draw from.

SET THE PACE

Imagine your favourite piece of slow music played really fast, or vice versa. Worse, imagine all the music you ever listened to played at the same tempo throughout. Getting the pace just right is extremely important. Handled properly it:

♦ enhances the atmosphere
♦ matches and underlines characters' moods
♦ advances or delays the action appropriately
♦ changes fairly frequently.

The last point can be a particular stumbling block. No matter how skilful the writing, too much delivered at the same speed can leave us feeling like a refugee from the January sales, or the recipient of a long sermon with no hard pew to keep us awake. Cinema and television with their ever shorter scenes and frequent changes of pace have no doubt influenced our tastes in this respect.

Study the structure
Watch your chosen video with the above criteria in mind.

♦ Pick some scenes where atmosphere is particularly important. What effect does the pace of those scenes have on their atmosphere?

♦ Note the way pace is matched to the main characters' mood. Could this have been done differently?

♦ Select a 20-minute passage. Note the length and tempo of each scene within it. What is the proportion of fast to slow/short to longer scenes?

◆ Select a section of your chosen book to study in the same way.

CASE STUDY

David enjoyed working analytically with both the screenplay and the video of 'Witness'. He then spent the best part of a week analysing *Forty Words for Sorrow* by Giles Blunt – currently his favourite crime novel. He felt this had really paid off in terms of what he learned about setting the right pace – an aspect which seemed to have eluded him before.

Focus on the words

Camera movement, actors' performances and soundtrack all help to set the pace on screen. A novelist, journalist or storywriter has only words on paper through which to convey this vital element. Some writers come unstuck because they recall the fervour or languor with which they wrote, and therefore believe these have been committed to the page.

Masterly handling of pace leaves no doubt as to the author's intentions. Compare these extracts from Virginia Woolf's novel *The Waves*. Read them aloud several times as you study them.

First, the opening:

'The sun had not yet risen. The sea was indistinguishable from the sky, except that the sea was slightly creased as if a cloth had wrinkles in it. Gradually as the sky whitened a dark line lay on the horizon dividing the sea from the sky and the grey cloth became barred with thick strokes moving, one after another, beneath the surface, following each other, pursuing each other perpetually.'

The rhythm of this extract is like the in and out of the sea itself. It is almost impossible to read it any other way, or to hurry it. How is this achieved?

♦ Using this extract as a guide, create a descriptive piece with a similar tempo.

Later, the early morning sea is described:

'(The sun)bared its face and looked straight over the waves. They fell with a regular thud. They fell with the concussion of horses' hooves on the turf. Their sprays rose like the tossing of lances and assegais over the riders' heads. They swept the *beach with steel blue and diamond-tipped water. They drew in and out with the energy, the muscularity, of an engine which sweeps its force in and out again.'*

About half-way through the book, the afternoon sea is described:

'The waves massed themselves, curved their backs and crashed. Up spurted stones and shingle. They swept round the rocks, and the spray, leaping high, spattered the walls of a cave that had been dry before, and left pools inland, where some fish stranded lashed its tail as the wave drew back.'

The vitality of the images in the second two extracts defy us to read them meditatively – but that is just one element of the craftsmanship. Notice the shorter sentences, and the way commas are used to break longer ones into short bites to hurry us along.

(What might an inner-critic style English teacher say about commas between 'swept round the rocks, and the spray, leaping high', and none in the phrase 'where some fish stranded lashed its tail'?)

◆ Write a sequel to your first descriptive piece, using short sentences and 'unorthodox' commas to create urgency.

Use of the present participle ('ing' suffix), tends to slow down action. In the first extract there are four examples, in each of the others only one. The first extract uses only two images; the cloth and the lines, both of which are introduced slowly. Description is mainly in the passive voice: 'the sea *was indistinguishable . . . was slightly creased*', 'the grey cloth *became barred*'. There is a dream-like detachment: '*as if a cloth had wrinkles in it*' rather than 'like a wrinkled cloth'. Later the sea becomes a cloth and, as in a dream, we do not question it.

◆ Read the first extract again. For the present participles, substitute 'which divided . . . which moved, followed, pursued'. Compare the effect. How many present participles did you use in your first descriptive piece? How much did you use the passive voice? Can you develop this further?

In complete contrast, the second and third extracts overflow with vigorously active images, which follow each other rapidly. In the second extract these are highly focused. It is like being overtaken by the cavalry at full charge. We hear hooves, see weapons, riders – with 'the energy, the muscularity, of an engine'. In the third extract we are thrown from image to image; the waves, stones and shingle, rocks, spray, the walls of a cave. It feels like a performance of the 1812 Overture, complete with manic conductor in danger of being cut off by the tide.

◆ Develop your second descriptive piece further, introducing more images, using the active voice and limiting the use of present participles.

Focus on the sounds

Speech, like writing, is physical. Some sounds are less complex and easier to produce than others. 'M', one of the first consonants a baby learns to pronounce, is easy. So are 'B' and 'W'. They use natural lip positions. 'V', on the other hand, requires a tricky movement of the lower lip, and may be pronounced as 'W' in the early years. 'K' and 'G' require co-ordination of tongue and soft palate. Short vowel sounds require least work from the larynx.

Most can be 'grunted' with lips hanging loose; a – e – u – try it. Long vowels require more effort, and most diphthongs require this effort to be co-ordinated with tongue and lip movement.

Writers need to be aware of these relative complexities because the harder a sound is to make, the longer it takes to pronounce – and this affects pace. Even when we read silently, the brain carries on transmitting 'how to' messages to the brain. Some people's lips move as they read. Most people's larynxes respond, however subtly.

Experiment with sounds

◆ Place your fingertips lightly on your Adam's apple and try some short vowel sounds followed by 'ou', 'oi', 'oo'. Try reading silently and notice any subtle movements of the larynx as you do so.

◆ Try all the consonants, noticing which ones require the most complex movements of the speech apparatus. (Those which require co-ordinated release of air – 'f', 'p', 'sh', etc. are short sounds because they are explosive.)

- Read the Virginia Woolf extracts aloud in the light of these findings.

- Read a slow and a fast passage from your chosen book aloud, noticing what is happening to your speech apparatus as you do so.

Because we are accustomed to these physically imposed rhythms, we usually sort them naturally as we write. However, it is good to have them in mind when we analyse our work. 'Do I need more explosive consonants. Would longer vowel sounds work better here?' Such 'brush-strokes' can make all the difference.

CASE STUDY

Learning about how various sounds are formed, really appealed to David's analytical mind. He has set himself the challenge of using this knowledge in a detective story, both subliminally, in the sounds he chooses to set the pace and mood and overtly by including it as part of the plot.

Checklist

Pace is affected by:

- sentence length
- use of punctuation
- use of active or passive voice
- use of present participles
- number of images and their speed of presentation
- length of sounds involved in speaking the words.

GET INTO A MOOD

This title is chosen deliberately to express the fact that we cannot adequately convey a character's mood without experiencing it as we write. We can either start 'cold' and let the mood take us over as the words come together, or we can develop the mood within ourselves first and let the words flow from there. Many actors favour the latter approach, drawing on specific personal memories to help them portray emotion on stage. It is this approach that we will be using here, with the aid of guided visualisations.

Before starting, there is an important question to be considered. What do you do with this mood and these emotions afterwards? If the mood is a positive one, you may want to stay with it. If not, you will need to de-role. Sometimes you can do this by firmly stating your name (in other words stating that you are not the character you have been portraying). Turning to some familiar household task or talking to a friend can also help. If the mood has taken over, you may need to repeat the visualisation that took you into it, substituting positive memories for oppressive ones. Revisiting difficult times takes courage. It should be avoided if currently under emotional stress.

CASE STUDY

Karen had a persistent feeling of sadness which she was unable to explain. She told the writing group that when her boss had spoken abruptly that morning, she had burst into tears. Karen had mentioned on a previous occasion that her teenage years were quite difficult. One of the other students reminded her that she was currently writing a story about a troubled teenager. This experience helped her to recognise how vulnerable she is in some areas. She is learning to take care of herself emotionally when she writes. She always de-roles now, and often 'takes the Grail Maiden with her' as a companion in visualisations.

Assuming you are not feeling fragile or that the mood you wish to explore is a positive one, the following visualisations should be taped and worked with in the usual way (see Chapter 2).

EXERCISE

Guided visualisation 1: Mood sampling – energetic/tired

Close your eyes. Imagine yourself at the sea on a bracing day in early Summer.

The sun is shining on the sea and it is also quite windy. The waves are crashing in. You can feel the wind whipping spray into your face.

Choose whether you want to go for a swim, or an invigorating walk along the front. Allow this image to fade.

Now turn your attention inwards – perhaps you are feeling a little tired just now – a little low in energy. So just let an image for that tiredness appear.

Let that image talk to you, and tell you how it feels . . . and what do you reply?

Now let an image for your energy appear . . . and let that image talk to you . . . What do you reply? Become tiredness and talk to energy . . . Switch roles – become energy and reply to tiredness.

Let this conversation between tiredness and energy continue for a while. Switch roles whenever you need to. See what you can discover.

When you are ready, open your eyes and make any notes you need to make.

Guided visualisation 2: Recalling a mood

How is your character feeling at this point in the story? Can you remember a time when you felt like this? Recall it in as much detail as possible. Allow the feelings to increase in intensity.

Where do you feel this most in your body?

Concentrate on this place in your body. Allow the feelings to grow.

How big is this feeling now? What shape is it? What colour?

What kind of weather goes with this feeling? What temperature?

What time of day goes with your feelings? What time of year?

Think of a place that goes well with these feelings.

Allow an image of this place to develop. Explore it. Feel it.

Notice how it smells. What can you hear?

Notice objects the colour of your mood beginning to appear in this place.

And now someone is approaching. They are dressed in this colour.

They are carrying something which symbolises your mood.

Talk to them about it if you want to.

When you are ready, take your leave of this person. Return to the present and make any notes you need to make.

- How are you feeling? Make this the subject of a timed writing.
- De-role if you need to.

Guided visualisation 3: Mood reflected in the environment

Return to the place you explored in Visualisation 2. Give it a voice. Let it describe its feelings. How do you respond?

Search for the object which the person was carrying. Let it too have a voice and speak about its feelings. . . Let the object and place talk to one another.

Is there anything you would like to say to them? Is any resolution needed? Who, or what could help?

In the distance you see a stranger approaching. Watch them. See how they react to this environment. What happens when they see the object?

Make yourself known to this person and see what happens next.

Let the situation draw to a natural conclusion, return to the present and make any notes you need to make. ■

Writing practice

♦ Write for five minutes as the place, beginning 'I feel . . .'

♦ Write for five minutes as the object, beginning 'I feel . . .'

♦ Use both hands to write a dialogue between the two.

♦ Write for five minutes as the stranger.

♦ Describe in one word the main feeling you have been exploring? Make it the centre of a web.

♦ Use the web to help you describe your character's mood.

♦ De-role if you need to.

Zubin found that his experiments with paint worked on his mood as well as helping him to create a sense of atmosphere. He brought art materials to the class the following week so that we could try it. We replaced timed writing with timed painting that session, and found it very effective. In the first instance, at Zubin's recommendation, we painted freely to music for fifteen minutes. Then, as a group, we discussed the moods and feelings we had evoked. Finally we explored and developed these moods individually, either in paint or words, or both. Even those who considered themselves to be 'no good at art', found they were able to produce something which both pleased and inspired them. Many students have added this approach to their regular routine as a result.

Writing experiments

Using what you have discovered in this chapter, explore atmosphere and mood further by experimenting with different paces.

Try:

- ◆ slow and fast: happiness, terror, supermarket
- ◆ a slow-motion rush hour
- ◆ inner turmoil/outer calm and vice versa.

It is important to bear in mind that a character's mood is likely to affect us as we write. When this happens we should de-role, or do something different which will change our mood, or reverse the entire process by evoking a new mood and writing from that. Writing can sometimes be a lonely occupation and we need to take care of ourselves. Please remember that it is unwise to evoke difficult emotions when under stress.

5

Work with Beginnings and Endings

START WITH A BANG

There are beginnings that will not be ignored. Once read they stay with you, compel you to return, to read on. Some are intriguing:

♦ 'Time is not a line but a dimension, like the dimensions of space. If you can bend space, you can bend time also, and if you knew enough and could move faster than light you could travel backwards in time and exist in two places at once.'

(Margaret Atwood: *Cat's Eye*)

♦ 'As a baby, Tom Avery had twenty-seven mothers. So he says. Ask me more, his eyes beg, ask me for details.
Well, then.'

(Carol Shields: *Republic of Love*)

♦ 'It was seven minutes after midnight. The dog was lying on the grass in the middle of the lawn in front of Mrs. Shears' house. Its eyes were closed. It looked as if it was running on its side, the way dogs run when they think they are chasing a cat in a dream. But the dog was not running or asleep. The dog was dead.'

(Mark Haddon: *The Curious Incident of the Dog in the Night-time*)

Some are bizarre or surreal:

♦ 'While Pearl Tull was dying, a funny thought occurred to her.'

(Anne Tyler: *Dinner at the Homesick Restaurant*)

+ 'You are about to begin reading Italo Calvino's new novel, *If on a winter's night a traveller.*'

(Italo Calvino: *If on a winter's night a traveller*)

+ 'In the first shop they bought a packet of dogseed, because Doreen had always wanted to grow her own dog.'

(Jeff Noon: *pixel juice*)

Some strike a chord deep within us:

+ 'I exist! I am conceived to the chimes of midnight on the clock on the mantelpiece in the room across the hall.'

(Kate Atkinson: *Behind the Scenes at the Museum*)

Some are shocking:

+ 'All of us walk around naked. The delousing is finally over, and our striped suits are back from the tanks of Cyclone B solution, an efficient killer of lice in clothing, and of men in gas chambers.'

(Tadeusz Borowski: *This Way for the Gas, Ladies and Gentlemen*)

Some make us think:

+ 'Say a man catches a bullet through his skull in somebody's war, so where's the beginning of that?'

(Matthew Kneale: *English Passengers*)

Some plunge us into the middle of the action before we have time to think:

+ 'He – for there could be no doubt of his sex, though the fashion of the time did something to disguise it – was in the act of slicing at the head of a Moor which swung from the rafters.'

(Virginia Woolf: *Orlando*)

or even into the middle of a conversation:

◆ 'Yes, of course, if it's fine tomorrow,' said Mrs Ramsay. 'But you'll have to be up with the lark, she added.'

(Virginia Woolf: *To the Lighthouse*)

The prize for the cleverest beginning ever should probably go to Adam Thorpe for the opening of *Still*. No more can be said about it without spoiling the impact. Experience it yourself if you have not done so already.

As well as hooking the reader's attention, the above beginnings serve another important purpose, i.e. revealing what kind of story this is going to be. In *How to Write a Million*, Orson Scott Card describes the opening paragraphs of a story as 'an implicit contract with the reader' whereby that reader 'knows what to expect, and holds the thread of that structure throughout the tale.' In each of the examples given, the expectations raised by the opening are fulfilled as the story unfolds (or not fulfilled in the case of *To the Lighthouse* – the theme of which is unfulfilled expectations). With just a few words, the authors caught their reader's attention and prepared the ground for everything that followed. How was this achieved?

In many of the above examples, we are introduced to the main character straight away, and that character is doing or saying something. This pulls us right into the action and engages our emtions – particularly when the character is named. In the examples where the character is not introduced in this way, there is good reason. In the Margaret Atwood passage, for example, addressing the reader as 'you' creates a certain feeling of intimacy, while the subject matter creates an impression of vast tracts of time and space – preparing the way perfectly for what is to follow.

Mark Haddon makes his 'implicit contract with the reader' by focusing on the dog, which is to become the subject of the narrator's obsession. Tadeusz Borowski in his opening statement, 'All of us walk around naked', evokes both the intimacy and the anonymity of the scene. He also makes a bizarre situation ordinary by describing it in a matter-of-fact way – which is what he continues to do throughout this extraordinary book. Matthew Kneale takes a similarly 'detached' approach with his 'Say a man catches a bullet through his skull in somebody's war'. However, in less skilled hands, placing the reader at a certain distance initially as some of these writers have done, could quickly lose that reader altogether.

Study a variety of beginnings

How did you react to that collection of beginnings? Did you prefer those that were intimate or those which were more detached? Were there any which particularly made you want to read on? Can you say what it was that you liked or that impressed you? If you did read on, did you feel that the author's 'implicit contract' with you was fulfilled?

♦ How would you answer the question 'What makes a good beginning?'

♦ Are there any differences between what makes a good beginning to a film, play or TV drama and what makes a good beginning to a story or novel? Take some time to think about this.

- Now return to the book and the DVD/video you studied in Chapter 4.

- Visualise the opening of the book as the start of a film. Take some time to really bring it to life in your mind – perhaps visualising the titles and imagining a soundtrack would help. Did it work for you?

- Now watch the first 5 or 10 minutes of the DVD/video. Write that opening as the opening of a book. Did that work?

- Think about why these transpositions did or did not work.

Study opening scenes in both performed and written stories. Note what does and does not work for you. What changes would you make to the ones you find unsuccessful? Try some more transpositions from one medium to another.

Select the beginnings of five novels to use in the next section.

Use successful beginnings as a starting point

Brainstorm
Take each of your beginnings in turn. Write the first sentence. Spend five minutes brainstorming second sentences.

Do some timed writing
Use each of your beginnings and some of your brainstormed sentences as a stimulus for timed writing.

Start a new story
Take a favourite beginning and use it as the start of a new story. When the story is finished, go back and write your own beginning. This is an excellent way to stop yourself agonising over your first paragraph.

When David realised his redundancy money was not going to last as long as
he hoped, earning something from his writing became a priority. He decided
to study some best-sellers and try to write in similar vein. With money very
much on his mind he chose Jeffrey Archer's *Not a Penny More, Not a Penny
Less*, and laughed out loud in the shop when he read the opening
sentence, 'Making a million legally has always been difficult.' This
was exactly the thought he needed to get started, and he finished his first
chapter surprisingly quickly.

Sheila has set aside a section of her writer's notebook for beginnings she
particularly likes. Whenever one catches her attention she records it. When
she is stuck for a beginning she often chooses one of these at random, then
alters it some time later during the editing process.

Another way is to use any traditional opening. Once upon a time
. . . Long ago in a far off land . . . There once lived . . . And it
came to pass . . . Dearly beloved . . . There was this bloke, see? . . .
Dear Mum . . . *anything* to get the words flowing onto the page.
You can write a more appropriate beginning at a later date.

ROUND THINGS OFF

What makes a good ending? Should it make you laugh – or cry –
or think? This will depend on the genre, of course. It may make
you shudder – as in *The October Game*, a story by Ray Bradbury
in which the horrible truth dawns with the last sentence; 'Then
. . . some idiot turned on the lights.'

◆ What endings have you found particularly memorable?

◆ Would you rather end with action or reflection?

Some of the most satisfying endings bring the story full circle, like a piece of music returning to its original key. Good examples are the endings of two of the novels quoted in the first part of this chapter.

- (Italo Calvino: *If on a winter's night a traveller*) 'And you say, "Just a moment, I've almost finished *If on a winter's night a traveller* by Italo Calvino."'

- (Kate Atkinson: *Behind the Scenes at the Museum*) 'I am alive. I am a precious jewel. I am a drop of blood. I am Ruby Lennox.'

Some authors manage to sum up the whole story in a masterly final stroke. As does Anita Brookner in *Hotel du Lac*:

- '. . . she wrote "Coming home." But, after a moment, she thought that this was not entirely accurate and, crossing out the words "Coming home," wrote simply, "Returning."'

Margaret Atwood, in *Cat's Eye* (see beginning of chapter) manages to bring the story full circle *and* sum it up in an extraordinarily poignant final paragraph:

- 'Now it's full night, clear, moonless and filled with stars, which are not eternal as was once thought, which are not where we think they are. If they were sounds, they would be echoes, of something that happened millions of years ago: a word made of numbers. Echoes of light, shining out of the midst of nothing.

   It's old light, and there's not much of it. But it's enough to see by.'

Study endings

Return to the book and video you studied in Chapter 4. Study the endings of both. Do they fit any of the categories of ending mentioned above?

Transpose them, as before. Does this work?

Again, study performed and written work, this time focusing on endings. Note what works, what does not, and any changes that could be made. Try some more transpositions.

Select the final sentences of five novels to use in the next section.

Start at the end and work backwards

Brainstorm

Take each of your final sentences in turn. Spend five minutes brainstorming possible penultimate sentences for each one.

Do some timed writing

Use each of your final sentences and some of your brainstormed sentences as *the ending toward which your timed writing is heading.* (You are probably practised enough by now to sense when the buzzer is going to sound.)

Create a new story

Similarly, take a favourite beginning and write towards it to create a new story. When the story is finished, write your own ending.

Unfortunately traditional endings do not provide the same impetus as traditional beginnings: The End . . . That's all folks . . . Here endeth the lesson . . . Thank you and goodnight . . . R.I.P. . .

Yours sincerely. These do not have the same energy raising qualities. You may disagree.

FILL IN THE MIDDLE

Write each of the opening and closing sentences you have been studying, on separate strips of paper. Choose one of each unseen, and write for 15 minutes, creating a narrative which will join that beginning to that ending.

For example, using quotations from this chapter, you might choose as the first sentence: ' "Yes, of course, if it's fine tomorrow," said Mrs Ramsay' and as the last 'Then . . . some idiot turned on the lights.' The task would be to write a story in between that made sense.

◆ Work your way through several pairings.
◆ Use the beginnings as endings and vice versa.

When you have finished, go through your narratives and highlight any ideas or phrases you could use in future. This is a good way to create the outline of a new story. Use some of the techniques from previous chapters to develop those narratives which show particular promise.

◆ Choose one of your narratives and develop it into a satisfying story.

◆ Pay particular attention to dialogue. How can this be used to move the story forward?

NB Unless you find dialogue particularly easy to write, it is a good idea to use 'dummy dialogue' in your first drafts, i.e.

dialogue which conveys the required information, but is not yet crafted or personalised. This enables you to move ahead without interrupting the flow of ideas. You can polish your dummy dialogue as part of the editing process.

TRY DIFFERENT ROUTES

So far we have worked with beginnings and endings in their fully crafted form. We can work in similar ways with opening and closing themes:

Opening themes
◆ The hero/heroine sets out to find true love/seek fame and fortune/ right a terrible wrong.
◆ Somebody is kidnapped/murdered.
◆ An injustice or grave misunderstanding occurs.
◆ The person in authority dies or leaves and someone must take charge.
◆ A new arrival upsets the status quo.
◆ There is an accident.
◆ Something of great importance is found to be missing.
◆ It is the only daughter's wedding day.

Closing themes
◆ Honour is satisfied.
◆ Honour is not satisfied.
◆ The conflict is resolved.
◆ Life is unfair.
◆ Characters get the happiness they deserve.
◆ Characters get their revenge.
◆ Revenge is not necessarily sweet.
◆ A 'quiet type' surprises everyone.

Brainstorm your own opening and closing themes and keep them for use when needed. Work with them as you have worked with the crafted beginnings in this chapter – make them the subject of timed writing, use them in random pairs, start with a closing theme and work towards the beginning and so on. Other ways of using beginnings and endings will be explored in some of the chapters which follow.

Other starting points

Use the following as beginnings, then discard them – or not, as appropriate. Or you could use them as the inspiration which starts you off, without reproducing them on the page.

- An overheard remark.
- A notice or headline.
- A small ad in the local paper.
- A proverb, or tongue-in-cheek version of a proverb.
- A sentence picked from a book opened at random.
- The first sentence you hear on turning on the TV or radio.
- A line from a song.

CASE STUDY

As Karen was queuing at the supermarket, she heard a man say, 'I wish I hadn't left my glasses by the bed.' This set her imagination racing.

Whose bed? Why did he take his glasses off? What chain of events was set in motion when he left them behind? How did he get them back? If he had a wife, what effect did this have on her? She tackled these questions in her timed writing, and is using the results to write a collection of poems which she plans to call 'I Spy'.

Which is your usual starting point – a beginning, an ending, or a general idea? Maybe it's a setting or a character – or something else entirely (like Karen's chance hearing in the supermarket queue). It is important to be aware of your preferred ways of working so that you can build on them. It is also important to be aware of alternative approaches so that you can try them out if you find yourself struggling or stuck.

CASE STUDY

As an aspiring crime writer, David's first step was usually to work out his ending. Beginning with the opening sentence of that Jeffrey Archer novel was a completely new approach for him, and he found it really worked.

Checklist

◆ Is your beginning truly compelling? Does it draw the reader in?

◆ What kind of ending are you aiming for? Have you achieved it?

◆ Are you working to improve your skills by studying the way beginnings and endings are handled in various media?

◆ Have you tried using existing beginnings and endings for inspiration and later discarding them?

◆ Have you remembered to use 'dummy dialogue' in early drafts, so that the flow of ideas will not be interrupted?

◆ Have you tried working with themes?

◆ If you are not satisfied with any aspect of your writing, have you considered any other approaches?

6

Surprise Yourself

The activities in this chapter inject new energy into your work by introducing the unexpected.

WORK IN DEPTH

In the visualisations which follow, you will use objects of personal significance to help you work at a deeper level. Some of these objects will be used to 'time travel', rediscovering things you had forgotten. Some will be used to take you into new territory. Use them to explore your own life first. Later, you can adapt the text of the visualisations to enable you to explore your characters' lives. This can be done in two ways:

1. On behalf of your character. You as author look at your character's life.

2. As your character. You become your character doing the visualisation.

Experiment to see which you prefer.

When you first do the visualisations, bear in mind the advice given in Chapter 4. Do not work too deeply if you are under emotional stress. One alternative is to visualise the scenes as though you were watching them on a stage or on television (see Visualisation 4) This helps you to feel less emotionally involved. Or it might be better to wait until you are feeling less vulnerable.

In Chapter 4, Karen decided to 'take the Grail Maiden with her' on guided journeys. The Grail Maiden was acting as a *talisman* on those occasions. A talisman represents our own inner wisdom. It can be any person, animal or object which helps us to feel supported or protected.

In guided journeys a talisman can also offer advice and answer questions. They are very useful to have with us. Close your eyes for a moment and allow a talisman to appear for you. Ask this talisman to accompany you in these visualisations.

NB As these visualisations work at a deeper level, when you tape them allow longer pauses than before, giving your imagination plenty of time to explore.

EXERCISE

Visualisation 1: Backpack (useful when starting a new story)

You are about to start a journey. Will you journey by day or by night?

When you have decided, find yourself in a meadow, with your talisman. Somewhere nearby is the road or path which will start you on your journey – but you need not concern yourself with that at the moment. Sit down in the meadow and rest for a while.

You have with you a backpack. In it is everything you will need for this journey.

What is this backpack like? How big is it? What colour? What shape?

Open it now. See all the things inside it. Take them out one by one and lay them on the grass. Spend some time looking at all these things which were in your backpack. You may want to discuss them with your talisman.

(Allow at least two minutes pause here.)

And now it is time to leave the meadow and begin your journey. How will you travel? On foot, or by some other means?

When you have chosen your means of travel, you see that there are three paths ahead of you – one to the right, one to the left, and another straight ahead. Your talisman helps you choose the path to take, and you begin your journey.

What sort of landscape are you passing through?

Are there any trees, or other vegetation? Are there any people along the way? Any animals?

Do you need anything from your backpack at this stage?

And now you see that there is an obstacle in your path. Is there anything in your backpack which will help you deal with it? You may need to ask the talisman to help you decide what to do.

When you have dealt with the obstacle continue your journey.

And now you encounter another obstacle . . . and with the aid of the things in your backpack you deal with it successfully.

And now you see that you are approaching a mountainous region, and there is a mountain which you are going to climb . . . and there is something in your backpack which will help you to do this in an ingenious way, which you have never tried before. It is amazingly easy . . . and before long you have reached the top.

Stand looking down at the path you have taken. You can see the two obstacles down there looking very small.

Talk with your talisman about other ways you might have dealt with them.

And now it is time to return, so make your way back down the mountain.

And make your way back to the meadow.

Spend a little time in the meadow reflecting on your journey, and the ways in which the things in your backpack helped you. Thank the talisman and any other beings which helped you on your journey.

When you are ready, open your eyes and make any notes you need to make.■

Use this journey as the subject of a 20-minute timed writing.

CASE STUDY

Zubin loved this visualisation and made it the subject of a series of huge paintings. The paintings inspired other students in the group to write further. Zubin now uses the visualisation regularly with his art students.

Use the talisman in your own way in the next three visualisations.

EXERCISE

Visualisation 2: Toy box (revisiting childhood)

Close your eyes – and find yourself in the bedroom you had as a child.

How old are you?

Spend some time rediscovering this room – the bed . . . the bed covers . . . the furniture . . . the curtains . . . the wallpaper . . . the floor coverings.

And in a corner of the room, out of sight, you now see a big toy box.

And in that toy box are all the toys that belong to you. Open it, and spend some time now looking at all your toys

(Allow at least two minutes.)

Choose a favourite toy now. Hold it, feel it. What does it smell like?

Let that toy take you to a time when you especially remember playing with it, or having it with you. Take a few moments to experience that time again.

When you are ready, choose another toy and let it help you to remember.

Choose as many toys as you want to – until you feel ready to close the toy box and return to the present.

When you are ready, open your eyes and make any notes you need to make. ■

CASE STUDY

Sheila was surprised at the power of the images and feelings evoked by the toy box visualisation. It was like being three or four years old again. She has used some of these long forgotten memories as flashbacks for a character in her new play. She is excited by the authenticity this approach brings to her writing.

EXERCISE

Visualisation 3: Wardrobe (revisiting your teens)

Close your eyes – and find yourself in the bedroom you had as a teenager.

Spend some time getting to know that bedroom again.

And now you particularly notice that at one side of the room is a huge wardrobe – it may be one you remember, or it may be much bigger.

And inside it are all the clothes you wore as a teenager, at home, at school, for different activities . . . Open the wardrobe now, and take some time to get to know those clothes again.

(Long pause.)

And now, choose one particular garment or outfit. Take it out. Hold it against you. Hold it away from you and look at it carefully. What does the material feel like? What does it smell like?

Now remember what it was like to wear it. Remember yourself dressed in it. How does that feel?

Let this garment or outfit take you to a time when you were wearing it. Remember what happened.

Try as many different outfits as you want to – until you feel ready to put them away again, close the wardrobe and return to the present.

Make any notes you need to make.

(You can also visit other decades of your life in this way.)

What will you do with these memories? They can be used in timed writing or a story, or to help explain something in your life that has puzzled you. You could also make the name of a toy or a garment the centre of a web. ■

CASE STUDY

Shamina and Karen found this visualisation particularly powerful. It eventually prompted them to make a collection of all the photos they could find from their teenage years, and to share the stories which went with them. This gave both of them a great deal of material to work with.

EXERCISE

Visualisation 4: Theatre of life (looking at a significant event)

Close your eyes – and imagine you are in a theatre. The curtain is down. The play will be beginning soon. This is to be a private showing just for you – and perhaps a few friends if you want them there.

The play is about a significant happening in your life. It will be in three acts. Act 1 will show the events leading up to it. Act 2 will show the happening itself. Act 3 will show the results of that happening.

Who will be in the cast? Where will these different acts be taking place?

And now, the lights dim in the theatre . . . the curtains open . . . you see the scene – and the characters . . . and Act 1 begins. Watch now as the events which lead up to that significant happening begin to unfold.

(Pause for at least two minutes.)

And now it is time for the curtain to come down on Act 1.

You may go backstage and talk to the actors if you want to, or you may stay in your seat and think or talk about what you have seen.

And now it is time for Act 2 to begin. The lights dim . . . the curtains open. What is happening? Watch as this significant happening in your life unfolds.

(Pause for at least two minutes.)

And now it is time for the curtain to come down on Act 2 – is there anything you need to do before Act 3?

And now it is time for Act 3 to begin. The lights dim . . . the curtains open . . . and you can see the results of what happened in Act 2 begin to unfold. How do you feel as you watch this story being told?

(Pause for at least two minutes.)

And now it is time for the curtain to come down on Act 3. How are you feeling at the end of the play?

Is there anything you would like to change – any scenes you would like to rewrite? If so, in which act or acts did these scenes appear?

You are invited to go up onto the stage now and appear in these re-written scenes. You can either play yourself, or one of the other characters. You can appear in as many scenes as you wish, in as many parts as you wish.

Continue until you have acted out all the changes you want to make.

(Pause for as long as required.)

As you come to the end of your changes, you notice that the auditorium is now full of people. You walk to the front of the stage and take a bow as the audience clap and cheer. Your new play is a definite hit.

When you are ready, allow the curtain to come down and the lights to dim.

Say anything you need to say to the rest of the cast, and take your leave of them.

Return to the present, open your eyes and make any notes you need to make.■

You might like to record this experience in the form of a play.

PLAY WITH WORDS AND IMAGES

Consequences (two group activities for 4–6 people)

EXERCISES

Activity 1: Sending your character out into the world

Each person will need a sheet of paper (preferably A3) and a pen. Fold the paper into 12 sections (in half, in half again, then in thirds).

- Think of a character you are working with at present – or invent a new one.
- In the first section, draw your character in a scene from your story.
- Pass your paper to the left. Take some time to absorb the picture you have received, then draw what happens next in the next section.
- Continue passing to the left and drawing what happens next, until all 11 sections have been filled.
- In the 12th section write the conclusion of the story.
- Retrieve your original paper and study the story which has now evolved.
- Take 15 minutes to write it.
- Read your stories to the rest of the group.

In the first part of that activity, you acted out symbolically what a writer does. You invented something and passed it on for other people to interpret in their own way. Our work is only partly our invention once it has gone out into the world. Then it also becomes part of other people's creative process.

◆ How did it feel to let your character pass out of your hands?
◆ How did you feel when you saw what had happened to your character?

Activity 2: Creating a bizarre situation

Each person will need a sheet of paper and a pen.

◆ At the top of your sheet of paper write an adjective. Fold it over once so that the word is hidden. Pass it to the left.
◆ On the paper you received, write a noun. Fold as before and pass it on.
◆ Now write a verb in the past tense. Fold and pass it on.
◆ Now write a preposition. Fold. Pass it on.
◆ Write an adjective. Fold, pass it on.
◆ Write a noun. Fold, pass it on.
◆ Unfold the sheets of paper and read out the sentences that have been made, inserting **a, an, the** where necessary.

Use some or all of these, probably bizarre, sentences in any way you choose.

Random words (group or solo activity)

You will need paper cut into 10 strips, and a volunteer (if working in a group) to act as reader.

Choose a beginning and an ending from different stories. Or choose two sentences at random. Use one as a beginning, one as an ending.

The task is to write narrative that will join one to the other, as in Chapter 5 – **but with a difference.**

- If in a group, divide the strips of paper among them. One word is to be written on each strip and passed to the reader. If working alone, open the dictionary, point to a word and write it on a strip. Repeat ten times.
- Begin writing. As you write, the reader will select a strip and read the word on it aloud (or you will select your own strip if working alone). The word must be incorporated into your writing within the next sentence or two.
- Continue until all the strips are used up.

Instead of writing words on strips you can use a radio, turning up the volume from time to time and using the first word you hear. This can also liven up your daily timed writing.

Random sentences

Poet Jenny de Garis introduced this exercise at a workshop I attended with some of my students:

Open any book or magazine at random. With closed eyes, point to a sentence, which you will then use as the basis for writing a narrative. Make each word in turn, the first word of a sentence in your narrative. Write with as little thought as possible – and no cheating! For example, supposing you were using the first sentence of this paragraph: **Open any book or magazine at random**. You might write: '**Open** up!' he yelled, hammering at the door of my hotel room. **Any** hope of sleep went right out of the window.

'**Book** yourself out of here right now,' he bawled 'or . . . '**Or** what?' I yawned as I began to hunt around for my dressing-gown. **Magazine** agony aunts would no doubt advise against leaving oneself open in this way, but I was past caring. **At** least he didn't have his gun this time, as I had it with me. **Random** thoughts as to how I might make use of it filled my head as I made my way reluctantly towards the door. ■

CASE STUDIES

Sheila decided to work with a sentence from a book she particularly liked, David Treur's *Little*. 'The sun that had been visible for weeks on end drew women from inside to the backyards so they could enjoy it on their shoulders and on their arms while they scrubbed the laundry.'

Here is part of the passage she came up with:

The thing about summer out here is – it's hot. Sun is the one commodity you can be sure of. That it is more of a liability than an asset to a fair-skinned Pom like me, has been the source of some amusement to my fellow workers. Had I known what I was in for, I would never have applied for this job. 'Been at the paint-stripper, mate?' they shout, pointing at my red nose and peeling cheeks. 'Visible at least,' I think ruefully, being the sort of chap people generally tend not to notice. For all they know, I could be another Singing Detective, suffering some horrible affliction of the skin, and this could be my usual appearance . . . Weeks can go by when jibes like this are my only human contact. On the plus side, it's predictable and I have learned to live with it to a certain extent. 'End all the anguish and come home!' my sister, Melanie, says when I phone her in deliciously snowbound Toronto. 'Drew out some money from what Dad left us,' she says enticingly, 'so there's no worries about the fare.' 'Women, theatres, art galleries, a comfy bed – they're all here waiting,' she continues when I don't reply.
From as far back as I can remember, Mel has tried to run my life, along

with the lives of half the neighbourhood. Inside, as a kid, I would crumble as she laid down the law, while outside I shouted and rebelled. To tell the truth, she was very often right. The trick was to take that right path once she had given up and moved on to some other project. Backyards, for example – they were one of her pet hobby-horses. So riled up did Mel get about the state of the neighbours' lots, she could near enough have incinerated the offending weeds and debris with her yelling. 'Could you have some consideration!' she would shout at some poor guy whose dog had up-ended the garbage can while he was at work.

And so on. The remainder of the sentence – which was an unusually long one – has been left for you to work with. Sheila found that this approach altered her style in a way she liked. Try it and see where it takes you.

Of course, it need not be fiction that you work with in this way. Here is a rather different response from Zubin, who chose to work from a cookery book:

'Soak the dried mushrooms in hot water for thirty minutes until reconstituted, and set aside.' (Nadine Abensur: *The New Cranks Recipe Book*)

'Soak up the praise, why don't you,' the old man said bitterly. 'The people love you, son.' Dried mucous rattled in his throat as he exhaled harshly. 'Mushrooms out of control – that's what it does, all that up-front stuff,' he said. 'One minute everyone's baring their soul, crying and hugging. Next thing you know, someone takes a thing the wrong way and there's a punch up – over what? Hot air, that's what! Water down all that straight-from-the-shoulder-stuff, son, or you'll have a full-scale riot on your hands.'

For the life of me, I didn't know what to say to him. Thirty years or more ago he became my mentor and my greatest inspiration. Minutes ago all that had changed and it became clear we were now on opposing sides. Until I could make my peace with him, I felt I couldn't continue with my keynote speech. Reconstituted Families was the title. 'And their rewritten histories,' I wanted to add now. Set all the cards on the table, is my rule of thumb where relationships are concerned. Aside from that, I pretty much go with the flow.

As a poet, Karen wanted to generate shorter pieces. She came up with the idea of using proverbs and making each word the beginning of a new line. Here is what she evolved from: *A stitch in time saves nine.*

A word if you will. Talk.
Stitch up the tears
in both your hearts. Let
time heal. A wise heart
saves every beat for living.
Nine times – that's just for cats,

Karen had other ideas about stitching differences into a patchwork and also about the Nine card standing for death. In the end she was happy about all but the last line. Can you help her to improve it?

Reversals

Clichés can be revitalised by turning them around. For example:

- 'Work is the curse of the drinking classes.' (Oscar Wilde)
- 'My senses were taking leave of me.' (Christine Miller, poet)
- Overheard in a pub: 'The young people of today don't know how to have a punch-up without enjoying themselves.'

We can also reverse frequently used phrases. A person with a strict upbringing might say: 'Other people's parents ran to meet them – mine met to run me.'

Describing a wimp we might say 'he never chanced a stand.'

A poet distracted by love might describe his beloved's voice as 'Music to his ears, but earache to his muse.'

Someone whose house needs rewiring might have 'too many fires in the iron.'

There is also some mileage in reversing initial consonants (Spoonerisms). For example, of a character who frequently burns food, we could say 'Everything is mist to his grill.'

CASE STUDIES

Reversals really appeal to David's sense of humour. He has thought up dozens of them and is getting together a collection to send to a greetings card company. He is also working at turning some of them into jokes for *Week-ending* and the *News Hudd-lines*, which might make him some money. That, however, is proving more difficult than he thought.

Karen used to be embarrassed about getting her words muddled, especially when she was tired. Now she often makes a note of things she says by accident. She has used these 'Spoonerisms' in her 'I-Spy' collection, which is becoming increasingly humorous – a totally new departure for her.

Checklist
Surprise yourself into writing by:

- exploring the past in guided journeys
- creating group stories
- injecting random words into your writing
- using reversals.

7

Work With Your Dreams

A DIFFERENT WORLD

In ancient times, dreams were thought to be sent by the gods.
When we work with them, it is easy to understand why. Dreams
are wondrous and mysterious. They offer messages and gifts. They
take us into a different world, with different rules – a magical
world that is likely to vanish like Cinderella's finery if we so much
as clean our teeth before writing down what we experienced there.
In this chapter we will learn how to enter that world with
awareness and bring its treasures back to use in the waking world.

It would be useful to start with a very brief introduction to the
pioneering work in this field done by the Austrian psychoanalyst,
Sigmund Freud and his Swiss contemporary Carl Jung. Their
work underpins all the methods and approaches I will be
describing in this chapter.

Freud and dreams

Sigmund Freud had enormous respect for dreams, and considered
his book *The Interpretation of Dreams* to be his most important
work. The hundreds of dreams transcribed in it make it a rich
resource for writers. Freud's studies confirmed his view that
nothing we have experienced is ever fully lost to us. Events which
are inaccessible to conscious memory, remain in a vast
subconscious store which can be tapped through dreams and
visualisation. Even the most trivial details are retrievable: 'the
wart on the forehead of a stranger' as he puts it.

Such details are truly 'gifts from the gods' to a writer. That wart might be the very thing that wins the Booker Prize!

CASE STUDY

One week, Karen told the class about her dream of a woman who had 'eyes like white marbles with tadpole-shaped pupils'. Sheila then remembered dreaming of 'amazing flame-coloured hair with gold flecks in it'. The following week Zubin brought in a painting he had done of a goddess-like figure with both these attributes. It inspired a wide variety of writing responses, including a poem about a fortune-teller from Karen, the first scene of a play about a sinister optician from Sheila, and the outline of a crime novel about the theft of some priceless religious artefacts from David.

Jung and dreams

Carl Jung also placed great emphasis on dreams. In the second half of his book *Dreams*, he relates individual dream symbols to mythology and alchemy. Again, this is a rich resource for writers. Jung gave us the theory explored in Chapter 3, in relation to visualisation – that all elements of the dream represent aspects of the dreamer's personality. We will be looking at a number of ways of working with this, later in the chapter.

In order to open himself fully to what a dream had to offer, Jung would start from the premise *I have no idea what this means*. To get to the heart of the image and extract its full meaning, Jung would say to his client 'Suppose I knew nothing at all about a . . . Describe it to me in the greatest possible detail'. This open approach is yet another way in which we can surprise ourselves rather than limit our possibilities to what we 'know'.

CASE STUDY

The group took this approach with Shamina's dream about a dragonfly, and asked questions to help her remember everything she knew about that creature. When she read back her notes, the fact that the nymph shed its skin several times below the surface before emerging into the 'upper world' as an adult, had great meaning for her. Karen looked up 'dragonfly' in the dictionary and announced that it had 'powerful toothed mouth-parts', which Shamina admitted also applied to her in certain situations. The group then helped Shamina to explore the characteristics of both 'dragon' and 'fly', in order to coax the maximum mileage out of her dream image.

USING DREAM EXPERIENCES

Keep a dream journal

Why record dreams?

The fact that dreams are so often forgotten on waking was one of the reasons Jung urged his clients to write them down straight away (an idea which seems obvious now, but was regarded as rather odd at the time). Another reason for recommending the regular recording of dreams was his interest in dream series. Keeping a journal helps us to recognise patterns and identify themes in our dreams – useful both for personal work and in using our dreams for story making. Particularly significant on both counts is Jung's discovery that when we work with a series of dreams, *later ones often correct mistakes we make in working on earlier ones*. This is a dramatic illustration of the interactive process which occurs when we give dreams our full attention.

The very act of keeping a special book and recording our dreams thoughtfully in it, lets the psyche know that we are serious, and the psyche responds accordingly.

How should dreams be recorded?

Most therapists who work with dreams ask that they be related in the present tense. This reconnects the dreamer with the energies of the experience, and makes the work far more powerful. The same principle applies when we use dreams in story-making. Recording them in the present tense puts us in touch with the energies and gives the work immediacy. Reading them aloud can also be helpful. Taping this reading and playing it back to yourself can be very powerful.

◆ While the dream is still fresh in your memory, ask: 'If this were a film, what would its title be?' Record this title and your reasons for choosing it.

◆ Are there any changes you would like to make to this dream? If there are, record them.

◆ Ask 'What happened next?' and continue your dream in the form of a visualisation. Or ask 'What was happening just before the point where my dream began?' Record your answers.

CASE STUDY

In David's dream he was looking out of his front window and saw a man walking up the path with a key in his hand. The man then opened the front door and walked in. At that point David had woken up in a state of alarm.

He offered the dream as a group visualisation of 'what happened next', with extremely interesting results. A long dead father, an ex-husband and an alter-ego all made their entrances and insisted on moving in. In David's own visualisation, the man was a stranger but was most indignant at finding David in *his* house. This gave David the idea for a mystery tale with a clever twist, which turned out to be a prize-winner.

Some people claim they never dream. In fact everybody dreams at regular intervals throughout their sleep-time, but the dreams are not always remembered. We can change this by actively encouraging the process, as described further on in this chapter. American dreamwork therapist Strephon Kaplan-Williams recommends recording your thoughts on waking each day, whether you remember any dreams or not. Like timed writing, this maintains the momentum of the process. The way in which you choose to organise your dream journal is a personal matter. You might record in a linear way or in chunks, chronologically or under themes. You might draw pictures, include cuttings, use coloured pens, etc.

A method I have found particularly useful for identifying patterns and themes, is the use of an A4 page-a-day any-year diary. In this I record dreams and, very briefly, significant daily events. This takes, at the most 15 lines. There are 52 lines to a page. At the end of the year I start again at 1 January, writing under the previous entry. By the third or fourth time round, patterns are very clear. The two-line days tend to be two-liners every year. The 15-liners may expand. Aggravation with the car tends to recur within a few days either side of the previous anniversary.

The computer crashes on the same evening as it did two years ago – and the dreams with certain themes tend to have their special times of year to recur as well. It is a weird and enlightening experience.

Checklist
Dreams:
- may be capable of putting us in touch with everything we have experienced

- may represent many aspects of the dreamer's personality
- are best approached in a state of not knowing
- may be forgotten if not recorded straight away
- sometimes occur in series, and these can be self-regulating
- are best related in the present tense
- occur at regular intervals during sleep, but are not always remembered.

WORK WITH DREAM IMAGES

Les Peto, author of *The Dream Lover*, compares dreams to the intensely real world of play in childhood. Like Jung, he recommends a wondering, childlike approach in working with them. He describes dreams as 'feeling-pictures – almost entirely silent movies, which rely for their impact on striking visual images, larger than life, surreal and irrational situations.'

He suggests listing all the images, then taking each one and saying 'This reminds me of . . .', writing down everything that comes, even if it seems silly.

- For a different perspective try drawing each image instead of listing them.
- Visualise yourself as all the different parts (as you did in Chapter 3), characters, furniture, the building or landscape you are in – everything. What do they have to say? How do they see you, the dreamer?

CASE STUDY

This approach really worked for Zubin. He had dreamed of what looked like multi-coloured walnut shells which, when he opened them up, contained exotic paper birds with amazing tails and crests – every one unique. As the shells were discarded, the birds came to life and flew away. He produced some wonderful drawings of these images and, when he went on to visualise himself as the different parts, recognised the conflict between his artistic self and the restrictions of his job. As the exotic bird he was longing to break out of the restricting shell, however colourful it might look. As the colourful shell he felt he was preventing his students – every one amazing and unique – from becoming alive and flying away. Sheila saw it differently and suggested that the colourful shell was keeping the 'bird' contained until it was ready to fly. It gave the group plenty to think about regarding artistic freedom and the demands of 'real' life. It also helped Zubin to make a breakthrough in making his first real attempt at personal writing – and a very powerful piece it turned out to be.

Work with one incident

Draw what happened

Recall a specific incident from a dream. Who are all the people involved?

Where are they standing? Where are all the objects placed? What are the surroundings like?

Draw the incident, making the drawing as detailed as you can. It will be like a snapshot or a still from a film.

- Using the present tense, describe exactly what you see.
- Describe the scene from the point of view of each person or thing you drew.

Show what happened

As above, but this time the scene is acted out, either in person or using objects to represent all the elements of the dream.

Fellow tutor Pete (who came up with the 'piglets crackling' in Chapter 4) was fascinated by dreamwork and brought along a dream for the group to act out. He related it as follows:

'I am flying around a Norman tower, which turns into a high-rise office-block. I stare in at the people working at their desks. I realise I am covered in gold. I am powerful. I am Mercury the Winged Messenger. The office workers run to the window, waving and cheering. I wave back. I zoom across the deep canyons between the buildings in New York, then suddenly I'm up in space, zooming around in blackness. I see a small black sphere with a bright blue aura pulsing around it and I land there. I see craters lit up by the blue light flashing intermittently overhead. Superman is there to meet me. He says 'Welcome to Phobos'. I am not Mercury the Winged Messenger any more. I don't know who I am. I'm confused and tongue-tied and shake Superman's hand, my arm pumping up and down heartily, out of my control. I zoom off, back down to Earth. A voice in my ear says 'A dangerous instrument!' Somebody hands me a Barclaycard bill for 2 billion pounds – the cost of my trip. I tell them I can't possibly pay – and suddenly I don't care.'

We had a wonderful time with that one, Pete himself playing the confused Winged Mercury, Zubin as Superman, Karen as the black planet with Shamina as the blue aura, and other members of the group as various buildings, cheering office workers and planet Earth. David played the enormous Barclaycard bill, which I greatly enjoyed presenting, instead of being on the receiving end. Everyone derived their own insights from the parts they played, as well as contributing to Pete's interpretation of his dream experiences. A lot of pretty wild writing was also generated as a result.

Take it on

After you have drawn or acted out your scene, draw, act or write the next scene.

Take it back

Draw, act or write what was happening just before that scene.

(Pete's dream provided a lot of mileage for these two activities also. Perhaps you would like to contribute your thoughts as to how he came to be flying around a Norman tower in the first place. Perhaps you also have some ideas about what happened regarding the 2 billion pound Barclaycard bill.)

What is missing?

Sometimes who or what is missing can give insight. 'I am looking for my glasses.' 'It was mid-day and the postman had not come.' So – what would you have been able to see if you had your glasses? What would the postman have brought? Or – what has happened to the postman on the way to your house?

Explore the mood of a dream

Spend some time getting in touch with the dream again. What do you feel as you remember it? Do you have an image for that feeling? What shape is it? Does it have a colour? Where do you experience it in your body? Does it have a voice? What kind of voice? What does it say? Focus on the feeling again. What would the opposite of that feeling be? Work with the opposite feeling in the same way.

Work with the body language

Gestalt therapy pioneer Fritz Perls felt that the message of a dream was best discovered freshly from within the self, not from an external interpretation.

He would often work with the body language a person used as they related their dream. Some of the techniques he developed were:

- *Do it more* – make the gesture bigger, faster. Make that sound more loudly. (Pump Superman's arm even more strongly.) This might help us to get the message the dream is trying to convey.

- *Do the opposite* – superman gives your hand a puny shake – how does that feel?

- *Finish what you started* – finish the kick, punch, caress, choked off scream, hair-raising car journey, or whatever.

What sort of dream is it?
The methods looked at so far will help you to get every last gram of value from your dream images.

It is also helpful to know what kind of dream you are dealing with.

In his book *Elements of Dreamwork*, Strephon Kaplan-Williams lists 24 major dream types. They include dreams which:

- reflect unresolved issues from childhood

- confirm the validity of our waking-life actions

- enable us to experience things not possible in waking life

- present issues to be worked through and resolved

- reveal accurately the dynamics of a close relationship.

Checklist
To get the most from your dreamwork:

- explore every image

- explore single 'snap-shot' incidents

- explore the feelings

- work with the body language

- think about what kind of dream you have had.

AWARE DREAMING

To encourage aware dreaming (and relieve insomnia) set up an internal dream sanctuary. Furnish it with things conducive to peaceful sleep: scented oils, soft lighting, music or silence according to your preference.

Imagine the softest of beds – perhaps a fluffy cloud which gently rocks. Spend some time imagining this sanctuary in every detail, so you can go straight there when you close your eyes. The process can be enhanced by music designed to slow the brainwaves – such as the *Delta Sync Sleep System* CDs from LifeTools.

Again, the *intention* to engage with your dreams is conveyed to the psyche because you have backed it up with appropriate action. The psyche will respond. Affirm your intention verbally, repeating a phrase such as 'Tonight I will remember my dreams'. Strengthen this affirmation by writing it down. Place a hand on your chest or abdomen and experience its weight and warmth. This helps to anchor your affirmation further. Don't be discouraged if results are not immediate. The most effective strategy is calm persistence. It will bring results eventually.

CASE STUDY

Karen had been going through a stressful period and this had affected her sleep patterns. She had not remembered any dreams for a long time. She started to work on an internal dream sanctuary, and also bought some sleep-inducing tapes. She slept soundly the first night she tried them, but remembered no dreams. The second night she spent time affirming an intention to remember her dreams. She dreamed of the Grail Maiden, and woke up feeling extremely calm.

Once you are in touch with your dreams, the next step is to indicate *what* it is you would like to dream and remember. Answers to questions and solutions to problems can be sought, including questions about your writing. With practice you can dream about your characters. Sometimes the next chapter or story gets acted out more or less in total – an amazing experience.

There are hypnotic suggestion tapes designed to achieve this level of engagement with dreams. I recommend Dick Sutphen's *Dream Solutions* and Paul Sheele's *Programming Your Dreams*, available from New World Music and LifeTools respectively. However, to reiterate, the most effective technique by far is *perseverance*.

CASE STUDY

Sheila had been keeping a dream journal regularly for many years, and had noticed how certain themes recurred. She had also noticed that high and low levels of dream activity tended to go in cycles. She had learned to wait calmly for the next high activity period, and not panic when her dreams seem to have disappeared. Since working with the group she has also reached the stage where she can get her writing questions answered during those active periods, and this is proving very helpful. She has found the hypnotic tapes particularly useful in getting the most out of this process.

Lucid dreaming

Lucid, or conscious dreaming takes the process a stage further by enabling those who practice it to know they are dreaming. The dream can be manipulated to suit specific purposes. For example, you could get the characters of your story or novel together and direct them in a specific scene. It takes dedicated practice to achieve this degree of facility. There are special exercises designed for the purpose. There are also devices, such as sleep masks which respond to the rapid movements made by the eyes when we are dreaming. A buzzer is activated which, eventually, is perceived by the dreaming mind and recognised as a signal that dreaming is taking place. Further information about this, and about lucid dreaming in general can be obtained from LifeTools, and awakenedminds.com.

Opinion is divided as to the merits of lucid dreaming. Some see it as a tool for inner discovery, others feel that conscious intervention interferes with the processes of the subconscious.

CASE STUDY

The idea of lucid dreaming appealed to David greatly. He bought a book on the subject and tried the exercises nightly for nearly three weeks before he started getting results. However, he has found his lucid dreams quite boring. The stories his characters acted out were less interesting than those he has arrived at by other means, such as timed writing and themed Scrabble.

Zubin, on the other hand, reported some impressive results – mainly with regard to colours and images which he describes as 'amazing'. He feels the process has enhanced his painting and sculpture rather than his writing, but believes the effects will be transferred to the latter eventually.

Checklist

We can learn to interact more fully with our dreams by:

- setting up an internal dream sanctuary
- making our intentions clear
- choosing the way that is right for us
- *persevering*.

(8)

Recycle

Sometimes a new character, setting or plot just comes to us. We wake up with a brilliant idea. We see or hear something that kick-starts our imagination. When this is not the case, try revamping 'one you made earlier'. Or revamp one that somebody else made – rather in the spirit of George Washington's axe. ('This is the very axe George Washington used when he chopped down the cherry tree,' the proud owner tells his visitors. 'Of course, it's had four new handles and three new heads since then.')

Amazing what a new head will do.

GIVE OLD CHARACTERS A MAKEOVER

Change one aspect

A single change can radically affect the whole picture. Other features become incongruous or find themselves in direct conflict with the newcomer. They have to adapt – or fight. Imagine: Henry the Eighth as a woman, Tina Turner as a village post-mistress, Ophelia in a bikini, Gandhi as West Indian.

Take any familiar character and try changing their:

- gender
- age
- nationality
- social status
- historical period

- occupation
- state of health
- style of dress
- marital/family status
- sexual orientation
- religion
- politics
- geographical location
- planet.

Changing one aspect is a very useful way of developing a character who is based on somebody you know – particularly yourself. It creates some distance, which enables you to see new possibilities.

Change a few aspects
Try the exercise again, changing two or three of the aspects. What effect did this have? How much of your original character remains?

Change everything
In the last chapter we experienced the effect of working with opposites. We can use this technique to invent someone who is the exact opposite of our original character (and probably represents their hidden self).

This new character can be used in their own story, or placed in conflict with the original, as in Robert Louis Stevenson's *Dr Jekyll and Mr Hyde*.

EXERCISE

◆ Use this short visualisation to experience opposites, focusing first on yourself.

Close your eyes. Become aware of yourself, your qualities, your feelings.

Think of three adjectives that you would use to describe your own character – the essence of you . . . take your time . . .

Now think of the opposites of those words. Become a person who has those opposite characteristics . . . what are you like now?

How does it feel to be this person? . . . What is your life like? . . .

What do you dislike about being this person? . . . What do you like? . . .

Take a little time to really get in touch with what it is like to be this person.

Now become yourself again. Open your eyes. Say your name out loud.

Make any notes you need to make.

◆ Make the comparison of these two experiences a subject for timed writing.
◆ Write a dialogue for yourself and your 'opposite self'.
◆ Repeat the exercise as a character in one of your stories. ■

Create the complete opposite
Choose a familiar character and brainstorm all the things you know about them. Now write the opposite of each characteristic you have listed, thus creating a completely new character.

- Get to know this character by using the tuning in exercises and visualisations from Chapter 2.

- Ask them to tell you their story.

- Write a scene where the original character and the opposite character meet each other.

GIVE OLD SETTINGS A FACELIFT

Changing the setting in this way is particularly useful when the subject matter of a story relates closely to something in our personal life. The setting where the original event took place might be so firmly fixed in our mind that we get bogged down. Making even a minor change enables us to move on.

Minor alterations

- Visualise your setting at different times of year, different times of day, different days of the week, in all possible weathers, in a different era.

- Use each visualisation as the subject of timed writing.

- Build a new house, school or supermarket there.

- Make a certain colour predominant.

- Fill the place with people.

- Empty it of people.

- Ask the setting how it responds to these changes.

Major rebuilding

- Brainstorm all the characteristics of the place. Write their opposites and use these to create a new setting.

- Transfer both settings from inland to the coast, or vice versa.

- Build a motorway beside one of them.

- Transfer one to the top of a mountain.

- Make one a tourist attraction because of its . . . (you decide).

- Build a new housing development or a factory.

- Visualise the aftermath of a disaster.

- Pull down buildings or put up new ones.

- Build a tunnel or a bridge.

- Employ an avant garde architect to make his or her mark on the environment.

Choose one or two of these major changes, and write as the setting, or as the change – or put the setting and the change in dialogue with each other. Make these personalisations the subject of timed writing.

Checklist

Create new characters and settings from old ones by:

- changing one major or minor aspect
- changing a few aspects
- creating the exact opposite
- introducing a new dimension.

NEW PLOTS FROM OLD

Work with the bare bones

In his excellent article 'Losing the Plot?' (*BBC Get Writing Website*) writer Mike Phillips points out that there are only a limited number of basic stories in any culture. He says 'Look hard enough at any story and you will always find the fingerprints of an earlier one.' In Chapter 3 we considered the three basic elements – what we might call the 'bare bones' of the average plot. They are:

1. conflict
2. character response
3. resolution.

In a love story these bare bones generally turn out to be:

1. Girl meets boy and there is an obstacle to their relationship.

2. Through the endeavours of one or both the obstacle is overcome.

3. They live happily ever after (*Cinderella*) or they part (*Brief Encounter*) or resolution comes about because of their death (*Tristan and Isolde, Romeo and Juliet, West Side Story*).

In an adventure story they probably look like this:

1. The hero or heroine set out to get something or prove something, but there is at least one obstacle in the way of their doing so.

2. Through courage, determination and resourcefulness (which may include wisdom in seeking help) obstacles are overcome.

3. The goal is achieved.

Once you have chosen a hero and/or heroine and an obstacle or obstacles, these bare bones can be fleshed out and recycled endlessly. Try a numbered grid like the ones we made in Chapters 2 and 3, heading your columns HERO, HEROINE, OBSTACLE and select them at random, then follow the three steps above.

Work with the basic form

Another way of recycling plots is reduce an existing story to its most basic form, and then give all the elements a makeover in the ways described at the beginning of the chapter. For example the story of Little Red Riding Hood can be broken down into these six basic steps:

1. A little girl goes to the woods to visit her grandmother, who is ill.

2. A wolf tricks her into revealing where her grandmother lives.

3. The wolf goes ahead of her and eats grandmother.

4. When the little girl arrives, the wolf tricks her by dressing up as her grandmother.

5. The wolf eats the little girl.

6. Her father kills the wolf, cuts it open and frees the little girl and her grandmother.

By using a grid, a dictionary opened at random, or just your imagination, you can change characters, settings and responses to come up with what appears to be a completely different story. Using a mixture of the dictionary and some imagination I came up with:

1. A famous actor goes to Paddington to surprise his lover.

2. A *Sun* reporter tricks him into revealing where his lover lives.

3. The reporter goes ahead and photographs the lover.

4. When the actor arrives, the reporter tricks him by dressing up as a beggar.

5. The reporter photographs the actor.

6. A policeman apprehends the 'beggar', causing the camera to fall and break open, erasing the photos of the actor and his lover.

A group of experimental novelists decided to recycle the basic steps of plots in a more complex way, and came up with the idea of branching narratives.

Branching narratives – simple version

Red Riding Hood is a good story to practice with, because it is relatively uncomplicated. Look at those six basic steps again. Now, to create a simple branching narrative, invent an alternative for each of the steps from 2 onwards. For example, in Little Red Riding Hood, step 2(a) could be *She loses her way and ends up at a house she has never seen before* – which would take the story along an entirely different route. Or, keeping the original step 2, step 3(a) could be *the wolf is a DSS Inspector in disguise.* As with changing one aspect of a character, the original is radically altered from the point at which you intervene.

If you were following this procedure for real, rather than as an exercise, you would combine it with a change of basic details (as in the previous exercise) prior to your intervention.

For example, intervene at step 3 in Little Red Riding Hood, keeping the the gist of 1 and 2 the same, but making the main character a little boy in a blue anorak on his way to see a friend. Have a woman trick him into revealing his friend's address.

Or, having intervened at step 3 and finished the story, write backwards from 3, inventing an alternative step 2 and a new beginning.

Or work backwards from either the old or new beginning – as in dreamwork when you asked what was happening before the dream began. What were the events in the life of Red Riding Hood or the boy in the anorak, which led them to set out alone that morning? A whole family saga could be awaiting revelation.

After you have made your alterations, the finished product will be unrecognisable in terms of the original – a real George Washington's axe-job.

Many short stories in women's magazines can be broken down and used as templates in this way (and many were probably devised in a similar way to begin with). Most have a fairly simple plot which would fit the six-step model.

Some stories are more complex than they might at first appear. Cinderella for example takes roughly 13 steps:

1. Cinderella's stepmother and her two daughters are jealous of Cinderella's beauty and treat her as a servant.
2. They receive an invitation to the ball the king is giving for his son, and are determined that Cinderella shall not go.
3. When they have left for the ball, Cinderella's fairy godmother changes her rags into a satin gown and glass slippers, and turns a pumpkin into a coach.

4. She sends Cinderella off to the ball, warning her to be home by midnight, when the spell will wear off.

5. The prince falls in love with Cinderella and dances with her all evening.

6. Midnight strikes. Cinderella remembers the warning and flees in panic.

7. Everything changes back except the glass slippers. One is left behind.

8. The prince orders every woman in the land to try the slipper, and vows to marry the one it fits.

9. The sisters lock Cinderella up and try the slipper. Their feet are too big.

10. Just as the prince's entourage is leaving, Cinderella escapes.

11. She tries the slipper and it fits. She also has the other one.

12. Cinderella marries the prince.

13. They live happily ever after.

(*War and Peace* is not recommended for the branching narrative treatment!)

EXERCISE

Simple branching narrative visualisation

Choose a beginning sentence. Write this sentence and then close your eyes.

Where does this first sentence take you? Take some time to get in touch with your surroundings.

Who are you? Take some time to get to know this character whose life you have stepped into.

There is a problem on your mind. What is it? Open your eyes long enough to write what it is.

This is the first place where your story branches. There are two things you could do about this problem. What are they?

When you are ready, open your eyes and write these two solutions side by side. Close your eyes again.

Choose one of these solutions. Picture yourself carrying it out. Picture this in great detail.

Suddenly another person appears. Because they are here, two things could happen next. What are they?

Open your eyes long enough to write these two possibilities side by side.

Choose one of the possibilities. Picture it taking place. Picture this in great detail.

Something is about to occur now, which will take you on towards the end of your story. What is it? As you think about it, maybe other possibilities will present themselves.

Open your eyes and write down these possibilities as they occur to you.

Close your eyes and choose one of the possibilities. Picture it happening.

Choose two possible endings. Open your eyes and write these two endings. ∎

Simple branching narrative with added complication

If the vehicle is a short story, it would be best to limit yourself to 13–15 steps along the path of one person's fortunes. If working with a longer form, however, we could at any point in the original or altered narrative, introduce a new element which would take the story off on a different route – resulting in a sub-plot, a lengthening of the original plot, the rise to prominence of a second character, or a completely new direction.

For example, after step 5, *The prince falls in love with Cinderella and dances with her all evening*, we could insert: *A messenger arrives from . . . Enemy troops are gathering. The prince must lead the army into battle to defend the kingdom.*

With no prince to defend her, Cinderella might be arrested after step 6 and languish in a dungeon until his return. Meanwhile we diverge from the main plot in order to follow the prince into battle.

Branching narratives – complex version

In this version every alternative step generates two possible next steps, building up a narrative tree as in Figure 6. Italo Calvino's story *The Count of Monte Cristo* is a branching narrative in which all branches are presented for consideration.

CASE STUDY

Sheila found branching narratives useful for making her plots more intricate and enabling some interesting sub-plots to develop – an aspect she found difficult to work with before. She has also noticed a gradual change in her style from using techniques introduced in our groups. She feels that visualisations have made her characters more rounded and her approach more subtle. She feels she can get inside the characters and tell their story as though it were her own. This in turn has boosted her confidence and encouraged her to try exploring these approaches further.

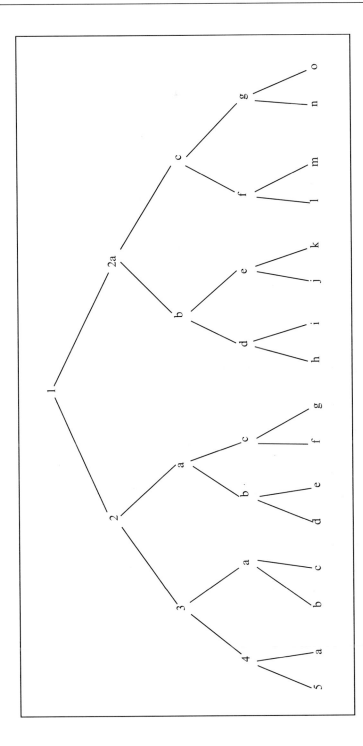

Fig. 6. Narrative tree.

Other story-making methods

The question game

Sometimes known as 'I had a dream', this game requires a partner. The partner questions you about your story/dream in terms that require a yes or no answer. Your response affects subsequent questions and a story gradually emerges.

The rule, unknown to the questioner, is that a question ending with the letter 'e' is answered with 'yes'. All others are answered 'no'.

Plot-generating software

These are mainly electronic versions of the branching narrative idea and range from the relatively simple and inexpensive, such as 'WriteSparks' to more sophisticated models costing several hundred pounds. (See *Useful addresses*, and and *ask for a demonstration* in order to be sure the programme suits your particular needs and style.)

CASE STUDY

David looked at several plot programmes, and eventually chose one of the more sophisticated. The basic principal is similar to 'branching narratives', which he also likes, but the programme generates multiple possibilities with little effort on his part. He was a bit concerned about spending the money, but feels it has helped him to put his novel back on course when he had been floundering. He hopes to recoup the money through his writing.

NEW TEXT FROM OLD

'S+7'

This is a method which originated with a group of French

experimental novelists. The 'S' may stand for *sujet* (subject). Sometimes it generates ideas for plots. More often it produces new modes of expression – phrases unlikely to have arisen from logical thought. Many people find it positively addictive.

You will need a small, very basic dictionary. The English section of a foreign language translating dictionary is ideal.

The method

Take any text. Begin to copy it. Each time you come to a noun, find it in the dictionary, count forward seven words and use that word instead.

If the word you arrive at is not a noun, change it to a noun. If this is not possible, move to the next noun appearing in the dictionary.

Alternatives

Change verbs and/or adjectives as well. Count a different number of words. Count backwards instead of forwards. Use nearby words if you prefer them.

Here are some examples generated from the transcript of a lecture on the novel.

Beyond the scope of literature became *beyond the scorpion of litigation*. This felt 'right' – the law can have a sting in its tail, etc. The phrase slotted neatly into a story about an acrimonious divorce. Later I was amazed to learn that astrologically Scorpio rules the eighth house which, among other things is concerned with law.

These narratives have one aspect in common. They are in principle verifiable became *These nations have one aspiration in communication. They are in prison vermicidal.* This is probably not usable as it stands, but could be developed in some way as a comment on the human condition.

I am dealing with a mistake or a fiction becomes *I am deathless with a mistress or a fiddle* – which went straight into a short story.

Many others – original sources forgotten, are filed in my writer's notebook. For example, *Fanaticism – a quiet glazed thuggery. A slimy new maggot abroad.*

Two simpering canines with a cephalopod curate between them.

A vaudeville of dailies reappearing on the polo marsh.

And one of my favourites, which never fails to make me smile: *Some of the oncoming goats were vice versa.*

CASE STUDY

Both Karen and Sheila became fascinated by S+7 and for a while they did little else in the way of writing. Eventually Sheila saw it as another form of writing avoidance and made herself stop. Karen continued to try it with a variety of different texts. When a friend came to baby-sit for her and Shamina, the three of them spent the evening doing S+7 instead. Karen finds that the sentences and ideas generated by this method, suit her style and she wants to make it one of her regular exercises.

Jenny de Garis's sentence exercise (see Chapter 6) is another example of creating 'new text from old'. If you find the approach helpful, try treating several sentences, a whole paragraph or even – if you are very ambitious – a whole story in this way. Karen took the proverbs she had been working on in this exercise and tried S + 7 on them. She felt it didn't work. What do you think?

Checklist

Discover new plots and new forms of expression by using:

- branching narratives
- an added complication
- the question game
- plot generating computer programmes
- S + 7
- the sentence exercise.

9

Craft Your Work

So far we have been exploring right-brain techniques mainly for the purpose of generating ideas and material. In the process, we have studied some aspects of crafting, mainly through drawing on internalised knowledge (e.g. using 'inner wisdom' and games of chance to construct plots in Chapter 3, focusing attention on the mechanics of speech production in Chapter 4, and studying our reactions to other writers and other genres in Chapters 4 and 5).

This chapter deals specifically with crafting. In keeping with the approach of this book, it offers a right-brain perspective on the subject – *perspective* being the operative word. The right brain puts things together in a non-linear way. Activities such as completing jig-saw puzzles, recognising faces and 'chunking' ideas are what it does best. Unfortunately, story-making is ultimately a linear process and this is where strongly right-brain oriented writers can come unstuck. Analysing, sorting, sequencing – the processes involved in shaping and styling a finished piece, are mainly left-brain activities. All writers, regardless of their hemisphere preference, need to master these in order to communicate effectively with their readers. Of course, it is in the processes involved in editing that the left-brain really comes into its own, and this is the subject of the next chapter.

There are many excellent books which approach the craft of writing in a practical left-brain way (see the reading list for recommended examples). Their advice can be invaluable, particularly for genre writers who need to master the fine points of particular formats.

A very good way of encouraging a happy partnership between right and left brain functions, is to use the approaches suggested in this chapter alongside those found in books with a more technical orientation. Eventually the two strands can be woven together – which brings us to the next section.

WEAVE YOUR MATERIAL

By the time you come to craft your finished piece, you will have assembled relevant material from a number of sources: writer's notebook, dream journal, timed writing, guided visualisation, tarot spreads to mention but a few. Some of this material will relate to characters, some to places, some to particular objects and some to feelings, mood and atmosphere. Having selected and sorted what you need, the task of weaving it all together begins.

As you weave character, place and mood together, tune in constantly to see how these various elements are responding to each other. How does the character feel about that place? How does the setting respond to the presence of the character? Which of them is responsible for the mood – or is it reciprocal? What situation might arise from bringing this person to this place?

◆ Try using each of the elements – character, place, objects, feelings, atmosphere – as symbols or metaphors for each other. How does this affect the dynamics?

◆ How is the pace affected by the language you have chosen? (See Chapter 4.) Is the pace right for the atmosphere or mood you are trying to convey? Is the language suited to the place and the character?

If the piece you are developing is part of a longer work, use the same interactive approach when weaving it into the main fabric. Dialogue with all the elements concerned. Treat the new piece as you would any newcomer to a group. Introduce it with tact and awareness.

◆ Now make the weaving process itself the subject of timed writing or of a short-short story (see Chapter 1) and see whether this gives further insight.

SHAPE YOUR PLOT

With certain genres, for example standard screen-plays, sit-coms and twist-in-the-tale short stories, the basic shape is set and the task is to write to it (some authors may disagree). Adopting this approach is rather like being given a recipe and assembling the ingredients accordingly. When not writing within a specific genre, we have choices about the form our work will finally take. To pursue the cooking metaphor; we look at the ingredients we have, and find or create a recipe which will make the best use of them. Many strongly right-brained writers are happier with this method. However, just as a hastily improvised recipe can let you down, stories that are insufficiently planned can end up going nowhere. Without a well-designed structure, all projects are destined to collapse.

Inner workings

'Begin at the beginning,' the King said, very gravely, 'and go on till you come to the end: then, stop.'

(Lewis Carroll: *Alice's Adventures in Wonderland*)

The way in which you structure your narrative affects the way in which your reader receives it, and is therefore of vital importance.

Within the basic structure of the plot there are, of course, many ways of telling the story, e.g. flash-back, implication, reported incident, symbolic representation, dream sequences, letters. In *How to Write a Million*, Ansen Dibell says 'All this structural hanky-panky isn't something to engage in just for the fun of it. Any departure from linear, sequential storytelling is going to make the story harder to read and call attention to the container rather than the content, the technique rather than the story those techniques should be serving.' She also advises, 'Make sure the running plot in your story's present is strong, clear and well established before splitting off to do *anything* else.'

When working out the structure of your story, constantly question your motives for choosing to tell it that way. If the answer is because it is 'original' or 'clever', you need to think very carefully about whether that is the only reason. If it is, you may be sacrificing other qualities – such as clarity – which are more important and might be better served by a more straight-forward approach. However, even straight narrative is fraught with dilemmas of choice. Should I use past, present or future tense, first, second or third person – whose viewpoint? These are often difficult decisions to make. Try an inner dialogue with the elements in question. Study the effects achieved by other writers. Keep the following guidelines in mind:

◆ If it is difficult to decide between first and third person narrative, think about the basic temperament of the character. Are they introverted or extraverted? Are they friendly or stand-offish? In other words, would they be happy to tell their own story, or would they rather somebody told it for them?

- Who is the audience? Would the character want to speak directly to them?

- If you choose present tense narrative, it is likely to quicken the pace. It is also very intimate. Are these the effects you want?

- Look again at the novel you studied in Chapters 4 and 5. Can any of the structural devices used by that writer be adapted to your purposes?

- How will your current decisions affect your last line or last idea?

Many creative people struggle with the idea of structure. It can conjure images of algebra, AGMs, tax forms and a thousand other things which render the muse dry-mouthed and dysfunctional. Novelist Alison Harding prefers to view structure as organic – an integral part of story-making, just as sentence construction is an integral part of meaning-making. As with the weaving process above, this shifts emphasis away from 'should' and 'ought', towards a more muser-friendly consideration of how the story *wants* and *needs* to be told. With this approach, the story is acknowledged as a living entity. The structure evolves as a result of inner dialogue with characters, setting and plot. Details are checked out as if compiling a biography. 'Is this how it was? Have I emphasised that strongly enough? Is this the best way to tell it?'

CASE STUDY

Sheila very much liked the idea of structure's being 'organic'. She is currently writing a play for the local youth theatre group, who have been working with the theme of 'Man's Inhumanity'. Much of the play's material evolved from improvisation, which has taught Sheila a lot about both dialogue and structure. The speeches are generally much shorter than she was used to writing, and this is influencing her style. In fact, on reflection she feels that this way of working has affected her whole approach to the project. There are numerous forms which our evolving plan might take. The first two which follow are models which Sheila tried when working with the youth group.

Try out different designs

Organise your notes

A planning strategy used by a number of writers is that of putting ideas, scenes, descriptive passages, etc. on separate sheets of paper and shuffling them around until a workable pattern emerges. Some writers blu-tack these notes to the wall, some pin them to a board or lay them out on the floor. Index cards are a more manageable option. Their size also encourages concise note-making. Several well-organised writer friends plan their work on index cards and file them, initially under topics and later under chapter headings. (Index trays long enough to accommodate a full-length play or novel are quite expensive. Sheila used shoe boxes – a viable alternative which cost her nothing.) Other planning systems – some of which may be used in conjunction with index cards – are suggested below.

Story boards

These are often used in planning screen plays. The sheet or board is divided into squares, one for each scene. In each square, everything the director or continuity person needs to know about that scene is noted in words or sketches. The end result is like an expanded version of the narrative steps described in the last chapter, and provides a valuable overview which enables any repetitions or omissions to be corrected. The method is equally useful to writers, both at the initial planning stage and as a means of keeping track of changes as the work progresses. Notes (on index cards or post-it notes) can be grouped on or around the appropriate squares.

If we take Little Red Riding Hood as an example again, at the initial planning stage a story board for that tale might look something like Figure 7.

Pictorial score
Musician Penny Gordon plans her compositions by drawing a linear picture that outlines the moods she wishes to evoke in the piece. She uses colour, pattern, and a mixture of abstract and pictorial representation. Underneath each sector she sketches her ideas in words and music. The pattern of moods in such a picture could be inspired by a painting, a piece of music, a poem, a specific event – anything which affects feeling and mood.

This approach appealed greatly to Zubin and gave him the impetus he needed to start planning his novel. As an artist he found his own ways of doing this, but for an example of how this mood-led strategy could be applied to story-making, see Figure 8 (and imagine the colours). This particular example shows how a story such as Red Riding Hood might have evolved from the ideas generated by such a mood-picture.

Like the story board, it provides a valuable overview of work in progress – as do the next three approaches:

Route map
Map the route of your story as if it were the Central Line on the underground, each stop representing a narrative step in the main plot. Show any sub-plots as auxiliary lines. Group idea sheets or index cards around the appropriate stops.

Red Riding Hood sets out	*Meeting with wolf*	*Wolf eats grandmother*
Describe temperament, appearance **Describe** scenery, weather **Atmosphere of wood** How is she feeling? Actions en route?	**Wolf's appearance** **Innocence/guile** – convey contrast through body lang/dialogue Wolf finds out where gran lives	**Sketch** gran's appearance **Emphasise fear** **Rapid conclusion** (Wolf remembers eating younger humans, compares?)
Wolf dressed as gran tricks RRH	*Wolf eats RRH*	*Rescue by father*
Innocence/guile **Dialogue** 'Oh Grandma what big ears . . .'	**Dramatic climax** **Shock** (wolf's open jaws from RRH's viewpoint?) **Sounds** Reader must believe evil has triumphed	Briefly refer to father's appearance – stress **action** **Shock** to wolf (axe descending from wolf's viewpoint?) **Father described** from RRH's viewpoint on emerging from wolf **Comfort. Relief**

Fig. 7. A story board for Little Red Riding Hood.

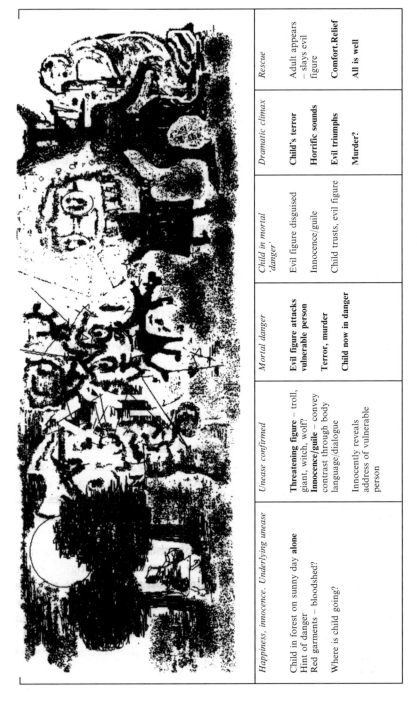

Happiness, innocence. Underlying unease	Unease confirmed	Mortal danger	Child in mortal 'danger'	Dramatic climax	Rescue
Child in forest on sunny day **alone** Hint of danger Red garments – bloodshed? Where is child going?	**Threatening figure** – troll, giant, witch, wolf? **Innocence/guile** – convey contrast through body language/dialogue Innocently reveals address of vulnerable person	**Evil figure attacks vulnerable person** **Terror, murder** **Child now in danger**	Evil figure disguised Innocence/guile Child trusts, evil figure	**Child's terror** **Horrific sounds** **Evil triumphs** **Murder?**	Adult appears – slays evil figure **Comfort.Relief** **All is well**

Fig. 8. Pictorial score adapted to story-making.

Topographical map

This type of map shows the location of key events in a story. Tolkein's maps of Middle Earth, and A.A. Milne/E.H.Shephard's map of Christopher Robin's world are well-known examples.

Some other layouts on which a story could be based are: a meal set out on a table, the plans of a house or garden, a musical score, a seating plan, a photograph, a game board or games pitch.

Family tree

The longer the work, the more comprehensive the drawing up of family trees needs to be in order to prevent chronological errors. A family tree can also be the starting point around which the story is structured.

Flow chart

Often used in computing, a flow chart shows possible paths through a programme or task. The Yes/No choices which have to be negotiated in using a cashpoint machine could be plotted as a simple flow chart.

The choices involved in self-assessment income tax forms would provide a far more elaborate example. A flow chart can be used to chart a character's progress. Unlike narrative trees, which give two choices at each juncture, flow charts operate on an 'if this happens, do this' basis. Also unlike narrative trees, they can jump several steps forwards or backwards, return the user to the beginning or eject them from the system entirely. See Red Riding Hood Flow Chart (Figure 9).

Instructions, directions and other sources of information

Stories have been based on recipes, menus, knitting patterns, the weather forecast, the ten commandments and train timetables to give but a few examples.

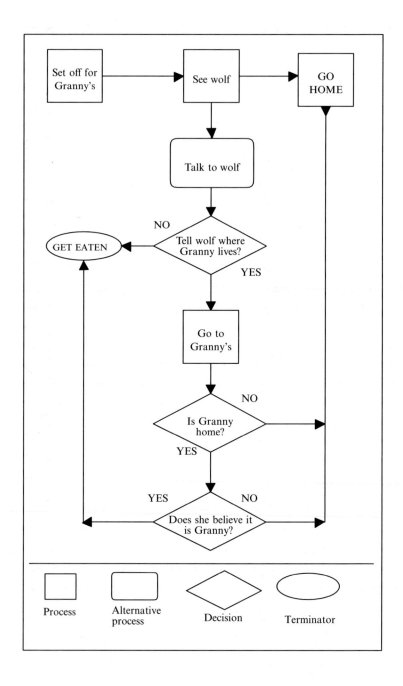

Fig. 9. Red Riding Hood flow chart.

CASE STUDY

David liked the idea of using ready-made structures in this way. He is currently working on the idea of basing his novel on the weekly profit and loss return kept by a detective to record the successes and failures of his cases.

Storage bases

Anything in which items are gathered together and viewed as a collection can be used as the basis of a story. A chest of drawers, a china cabinet, a library, a fridge, a shed, a sewing box, all have their story to tell. Personal memories associated with the contents can be evoked through guided visualisation (as with the toy box and wardrobe in Chapter 6). Or the story of the objects and the events which brought them together can be told.

Tarot spread

There are many tarot spreads, both simple and complex, around which a story can be structured. Each position in the spread represents the answer to a question, so that the spread can be used as a plan with or without the accompanying cards. (See Chapter 3, Figure 5 for an example.)

Write backwards

This is an approach used particularly when writing twist-in-the-tale stories and comedy sketches. In both cases the writer needs to set up certain expectations in the mind of the reader, viewer or listener in order to create the maximum surprise at the end. For this reason the ending is often worked out first and the rest of the story then 'written backwards' to a pre-determined structure. The techniques used in both genres are very specific and require separate study if this is an avenue you wish to pursue (see reading list for further information).

However, the idea of beginning with an ending and writing backwards from it can be applied to other types of story – as it was in Chapter 5. In that instance we brainstormed penultimate sentences, chose one, then created a new story by writing towards the new two-sentence ending.

This time we will work backwards step by step, first choosing a final sentence, then brainstorming scenarios which might have preceded it.

For example, some scenarios which might have preceded Ray Bradbury's final sentence 'Then . . . some idiot turned on the lights' are:

1. The boy opened the headmaster's drawer to return money stolen by his friend (then some idiot turned on the lights).
2. The men were standing naked in the middle of the women's changing room (then some idiot . . .).
3. A film containing vital photographic evidence had just been removed from the camera (then . . .)
4. The car's lights were wired to a bomb (etc.).
5. The woman thought the man in bed with her was her husband.
6. The funeral cortege was proceeding with dignity along the front at Blackpool.

Choose one brainstormed scenario, then one or more scenarios which could have preceded it. A scenario is then chosen to precede that and so on until the beginning of the story is reached. You then have a basic plot with which to work.

CASE STUDY

Karen emerged from her S+7 phase with what she described as a 'warped imagination' so that just the idea of 'writing backwards' had enormous appeal. She is currently exploring it in various ways. She also thinks the notice-board at work would make a good starting point for a short story, with dialogue based on people's comments as they read it. Poetry seems to be on her 'back boiler' at the moment, but she feels OK with that.

Checklist

When crafting work:

- blend right- and left-brain approaches

- tune in to various elements to see how they are responding to each other

- think of structure as organic

- choose an idea-organising system which gives you an overview

- check out other writers' solutions.

Also, if you want to write twist-in-the-tale stories or comedy sketches, you need to study the finer points involved in writing backwards.

FINE-TUNE YOUR CHARACTERS

- Study Chapters 2, 3 and 8 again. Use the exercises to get to know your characters even better.

- Use 10 x 10 as a safeguard against stereotyping.

- Study *Focusing on the words* and *Focusing on the sounds* (Chapter 4) again, to check that the language you have used to describe the characters really resonates with their particular personalities.

- Which actor or actress would you choose to play the part of your character? Imagine them in the role. Does this reveal any inconsistencies?

- Sit your character in an empty chair and talk to them. Change seats and reply as your character.

- Are there any questions you need to ask about your characters? Use the I Ching or Runes to help you find answers.

- If you have an astrology programme, look at the characters' natal charts again Look at their house charts and transits. Use synastry (see Glossary) for further insight into their relationships.

- Choose a tarot spread to help you gain further insight.

NB If there are tarot cards you particularly enjoy working with, have them copied A4 size and laminated. This can be done quite cheaply at most large office supplies stores.

FINE-TUNE YOUR DIALOGUE

Check that every piece of dialogue you have written performs at least one of the following functions:

1. Conveys essential information.

2. Moves the story forward.

3. Reveals the character and mood of the person who is speaking.

4. Establishes the relationship between characters.

Although the mode of speech provides clues to a character's era, geographical origins, and social class, dialogue should not be used to convey these alone. Dialogue that does not perform any of the above four functions should be cut. Skillfully handled dialogue can perform several of these functions at once. Work at making yours more economical in this respect. Check also that the dialogue is distinctive – that only the person in question could have said those words. If any section still sounds like dummy dialogue – i.e. anyone could have said it – it needs fine-tuning. This is very important to remember as the 'anyone could have said it' fault is an extremely common one with novice writers and is one of the most frequent reasons for having work rejected.

INVENT A PURPOSE

If you have no specific purpose for the telling of your tale, invent one. Do you want to make a specific point, raise awareness, entertain, shock?

Which particular sector of the population would you like to influence or affect? Having a specific purpose and a specific target audience in mind will help to focus your thoughts.

FOCUS ON STYLE AND CLARITY

Does your work sometimes suffer from 'stylism'? Do verbosity, minimalism and originality lure you like sirens onto the rocks of mumbo-jumbo? Does your internal critic then sail past with a loud hailer, shouting comments about 'trying to be clever' – and does your novel subsequently end up at the back of a drawer for another few months? Head for the calmer waters of Chapter 2 and *Tune in*. Inside is where your true writer's voice is to be found. Like structure, it is organic and can not be bolted on.

◆ Repeat some of the exercises from Chapter 2, then return to the piece you are crafting at the moment. The following exercise will improve both its style and its clarity.

EXERCISES

Pare down

Imagine you are have received details of a competition. The story you are in the process of finishing is just right for it – except that it is 500 words too long. Weed out the non-essentials until your story fits the required length.

Pare down again

Now write it again as a 1,000-word story – another very useful exercise in crafting. This time you may lose some elements which deserve to be kept, but you will probably have made a number of unexpected improvements as well.

Select the best

Select the best elements of your two shortened stories and combine them to produce a final prizeworthy draft.

Practice brevity

Make writing a story in 100 words – or even fewer (see Chapter 1) a part of your daily writing practice for a while. Many writers find this particularly useful when they are engaged in the editing process. ■

CASE STUDY

David hates what he calls 'flowery writing', with long sentences and a great deal of description. The idea of 'paring down' really appealed to him and he liked the idea of making his prose as sparse as possible, particularly the dialogue. The group agreed that his writing is much improved as a result. Zubin is rather fond of 'flowery writing', and did not enjoy the process at all. Nevertheless, he had to admit that his work gained in both style and clarity as a result of being what he regarded as 'ruthless'.

Checklist

◆ Use a variety of methods to get to know your characters thoroughly.

◆ Pay particular attention to the way they express themselves verbally.

◆ Focus your thoughts by inventing a purpose for your story.

◆ Reduce the number of words you have used to tell it.

◆ Reduce them again.

(10)

Edit Your Work

APPRECIATE YOUR LEFT BRAIN

As discussed in previous chapters, the right brain puts things together in a non-linear way. Its knowledge is gained through images rather than words. It can process many kinds of information simultaneously and make great leaps of insight. It understands metaphor, creates dreams and fantasies, wonders 'What if . . . ?' Such abilities generally receive less encouragement in the worlds of school and work than those which the left brain offers, e.g. logic, mathematical precision, ability to label accurately, order, neatness. One of the main aims of this book is to redress that particular imbalance.

However, this is not to suggest that the right brain is superior to the left brain. On the contrary, they complement each other in most activities. In fact after the age of five when specialisation of the hemispheres is complete, one cannot function efficiently without the other. A writer certainly could not function without access to the specialist activities of the left brain. It controls speech, reading, and writing. It recalls information and knows how to spell. As discussed in Chapter 9, the essential crafting and editing skills of analysing, sorting, selecting and sequencing are mainly left-brain activities.

The ideal is to get the two sides of the brain working in harmony, each supporting the other, doing what it does best while not getting in the other's way. LiteraryMachine is a software program

166

which claims to help with this process by 'structuring right-brain thinking'. (See *Useful addresses and websites*.)

The dynamics of your particular left brain/right brain partnership can be observed by returning to the hand exploration exercise in Chapter 2. How did the two hands react to each other when you first did it?

◆ Try the exercise again. Compare the results. Does either side of the partnership need encouragement? Is some negotiation needed? How do you feel about each side? Does your attitude need some adjustment?

A good working relationship between both hemispheres will make the strongly left-brain task of editing less daunting. Although the two hemispheres work together on most activities, their way of processing information differs. The extent to which they are involved at a given time depends on the particular task. Peter Vincent gave me an invaluable piece of advice. Never write and edit at the same sitting. He told me that when he starts work on a script he lets the ideas, however off-the-wall, flow from his right brain unimpeded. 'Anything can seem funny at this stage,' he says. At the end of several days writing he welcomes the good sense of his left brain which steps in to sort out what will or will not work. Before Peter gave me this advice, I frequently found that the processes of creating and editing got in each other's way and slowed my output down considerably. I found editing at a separate session so successful, that I organised my working week around it and now edit only on Fridays (plus the odd evening if a deadline is looming).

Confident handing over of the helm to the left brain in this way requires the services of a supportive rather than a censorious internal critic.

BEFRIEND YOUR CRITIC

In *The Creative Fire*, Clarissa Pinkola Estes uses the story of the brave dog Gelert (after whom the Welsh village Beddgelert is named) as a metaphor for the misguided critical process. Gelert, the King's favourite dog, is found covered in blood beside the upturned cradle of the baby prince. Thinking the dog has slain the child, the king kills him. He then finds the child unharmed beneath the cradle, next to the body of the wolf from which Gelert saved him. The wolf and the dog can be seen as aspects of our internal critic: the wolf a murderous aspect that wants to destroy the products of our creativity, the dog an ally, who wants to serve us and our creations.

Trauma, conditioning and poor judgement, can lead us to mistrust the dog and side with the wolf. Successful editing requires us to believe in the dog and to tame the wolf so that its power is harnessed for our purposes. As with the left and right brain, we can then develop a productive working partnership. The ultimate aim is to integrate and work with all aspects of ourselves in this way. A good starting point is to get to know both sides of the critic better through guided visualisation. This will work best if done in relation to a current piece of work which is at the editing stage.

EXERCISE

Guided visualisation: Get to know your internal critic

Close your eyes and focus on a current piece of writing. Which parts of it please you? Which parts of it are giving you trouble? What difficulties are you experiencing? Be as specific as possible.

Allow an image of your helpful internal critic to come to mind.

When you have a clear image, give it a name.

What sort of voice does your helpful critic have? What sort of things does this critic normally say? How do you feel about this?

Ask this critic to say what they think about your current work. What do they think about the parts you like? What advice can they offer about your difficulties?

Allow this image to fade. Allow an image of your negative critic to come to mind.

When you have a clear image, give this negative critic a name.

What is this critic's voice like? What sort of things does this critic normally say? How do you feel about this?

Ask this critic to comment on your current work – its good points and bad points. Has this critic got any advice to offer?

Allow this image to fade, and spend some time reflecting on the experience.

Which critic are you more inclined to believe? Which one do you like best? Which do you find more helpful? Will you act on the advice given by either ?

In a few moments you are going to bring these two critics together. Is this likely to cause a problem? If so, you could call on the mediating skills of a talisman, tarot character or other helper.

Allow these two critics to meet each other now. Encourage each to say what they see as each other's good and bad points. What concessions are they prepared to make in order to be able to work together?

Ask the two critics to discuss your current work. What changes would each one make? What arguments does each give regarding the other's changes? Allow plenty of time for this discussion to develop and join in when you wish to.

Before you draw this discussion to a close, ask each of the critics what they need from you in order to be able to work in partnership.

Thank them both for their help, return and make any notes you need to make.■

Checklist

◆ Right-brain thinking is not superior to left brain thinking. It is just different. We need to be aware of the specific skills of each side.

◆ Right brain and left brain work in partnership. We need to enable this process by recognising the contribution of each one.

◆ Our critic is often very useful at the editing stage. Fostering its positive aspects will make this process more productive.

CASE STUDIES

Sheila befriended her critic in a different and equally useful way. She was delighted to receive a letter from a producer who liked her play, but suggested a few changes. Sheila did not agree with all of them, but realised it would be in her interests to follow his advice at this stage. She studied his work by taping his latest play and buying tapes of others from the BBC. This gave her a good idea of his tastes and approach. She revised her play, resubmitted it – and to keep her energies flowing, immediately started work on the next one. Meanwhile there was still the youth play. After much editing and rewriting – particularly of dialogue, it was performed and received much local acclaim. While still on a high from this success, she received a phone call from the radio producer who had expressed an interest in her play. He was pleased with the alterations she made and wants to produce the play next season.

Sheila is delighted that her hard work and perseverance have finally paid off.

David is equally meticulous about editing, mainly because it is one of his favourite occupations. At work he used to be very proud of his concise reports. He now enjoys using the same skills in his fiction writing. He has finished the first draft of his novel (having abandoned the idea of keeping a profit and loss record as structure, but retained it as an idiosyncrasy of his main character). Ironically, he planned his work so thoroughly that very little editing is necessary.

Both Karen and Zubin, on the other hand, find it very hard to be this disciplined. They both dread editing and put it off for as long as possible.

As a poet Karen finds that when she writes fiction, a clear story line and an effective ending are aspects of her work which usually need attention. She often starts with a good idea and a great opening sentence and then peters out or gets sidetracked. Zubin finds his work often overflows with ideas and images that are not really going anywhere. When he and Karen do eventually get round to proper editing – often as a last minute joint venture – they are invariably pleased with the results.

PLAY THE EDITING GAME

The suggestion that editing can be seen as a game is made partly to reduce anxiety in strongly right-brained writers like Karen and Zubin, and partly to draw attention to the capricious nature of editing requirements. Unless you are in the position of being able to follow Polonius' dictate, 'This above all: to thine own self be true,' editing criteria will vary according to market, genre, and current taste. One editor will like your style but not your story-line, another the reverse. For one magazine your story is too long, for another too short, for another it is just right, but the heroine is too old – and so on.

Below are listed ten aspects of your work which will require scrutiny whatever your current criteria. Some general questions are asked under each aspect. As a focusing exercise, make this into an 'Editing 10 x 10' by adding more questions to suit your particular requirements.

1. The beginning
♦ Does it really grab the reader's attention? (If not, you could lose your audience altogether.)

♦ Does it intrigue, shock, strike a chord, plunge the reader straight into the action? (See Chapter 5.)

♦ Does it make you want to read on?

♦ Is the 'implicit contract' it makes with the reader a valid one? (See Chapter 5.)

♦ Have you read the beginning aloud to anyone and asked for their feedback?

2. Characters
♦ Have you brought them to life? Will the readers feel they know

these people and will they care what happens to them? (See Chapters 2, 4 and 6.)

♦ Are your characters authentic? Do their descriptions 'ring true'? Are clothes, speech patterns and cultural references right for the period and location?

♦ Is their behaviour consistent with their personalities? Is their appearance consistent? In longer works, continuity of costume and hair colour/style may need to be checked. A story-board is helpful in this respect. (See Chapter 9.)

♦ Do any elements of your characterisation need more emphasis? Have you asked anyone for feedback about this?

3. Setting

♦ Have you given the reader a clear picture of the surroundings?

♦ Have you done your research thoroughly? Are clothing, architecture, artefacts, cultural references, in keeping with the historical period?

♦ Have you checked continuity in this respect? Again, a story-board can be useful for this purpose.

♦ Have you conveyed the atmosphere you intended to convey?

4. Plot

♦ Is the story line absolutely clear?

♦ Could it be set out in narrative steps as in Chapter 8 or could you plot it on a route map, as in Chapter 9?

♦ Were any 'added complications' fruitful, or were they just 'clever sidetracks' which diverted attention from the main thrust of the story?

In the example given in Chapter 8, Cinderella languishes in a dungeon while the prince, ignorant of her plight, is far away fighting. The reader has the overview, which creates dramatic tension.

This path has many possibilities, e.g. having received no word from the beautiful stranger, the prince concludes she does not care for him. Eschewing love, he agrees to a politically sound marriage with a princess from a neighbouring kingdom. As the day of the marriage draws near, Cinderella tries to send the glass slipper to him but the ugly sisters intercept it. This all adds to the story's emotional impact. If the Prince had gone off to war and Cinderella had gone home and worried about him for a year or so, this would be a side-track. Other than a chance to reveal the strength of Cinderella's love, it would serve no dramatic function. In fact it would confuse the plot and destroy the story's momentum.

5. Story-telling vehicles

♦ Have you chosen the best way to tell your story?

♦ Have you used straight narrative throughout, or have you interspersed this with flash-back, dream-sequences, letters and other devices? What were the reasons for these choices – and were they valid? (See Chapter 9.)

♦ What tense have you chosen and whose viewpoint have you used? Do you have sound reasons for these choices? Might other choices be more effective?

♦ Have you used dialogue as a story-telling vehicle? What were your reasons for doing so? Was it always a good choice? (See Chapter 9.)

6. Dialogue

♦ Is your dialogue realistic?

- Is it authentic?

- Is your dialogue consistent with the characters' historical period, geographical origins, and social class?

- Is it distinctive? Could only that character have made that particular speech?

- Have you read your dialogue aloud? How does it sound?

- Have you checked that every piece of dialogue you have written performs at least one of the following functions:
  1. conveys essential information
  2. moves the story forward
  3. reveals the character and mood of the person who is speaking
  4. establishes the relationship between characters.

7. Feelings

'Proper structure occurs when the right things happen at the right time to create maximum emotion.'

(Michael Hauge: *Writing Screenplays that Sell*)

It is also important to remember that these 'right things' must happen to *people* and that these must be people about whom the audience cares. *Casualty* and *Holby City* are watched avidly by millions, not because they are about hospitals but because they are about people in crisis.

- How heart-rending or heart-warming is your story?

- Could your characterisation benefit from some fine-tuning to help the audience care a little more?

- Are the 'right things happening at the right time' – or are changes needed?

8. Pace

♦ Do any passages interfere with the pace you intended? Have you read any doubtful passages aloud?

♦ Have you checked sentence length, use of punctuation, use of active or passive voice and of present participles?

♦ Have you checked the number of images and their speed of presentation? Are these appropriate?

♦ Have you checked the lengths of the sounds involved in speaking the words. (See Chapter 4.)

9. Style

'You don't have to consciously cultivate a style. Just learn to write well and your style will emerge . . . If you peer too closely at your style you will end up parodying yourself. Your writing voice must flow from you naturally, just as your conversational voice does.'

(Gary Provost: *Make Your Words Work*)

♦ Have you 'tuned in', as suggested in Chapter 9? Returning to the exercises in Chapter 2 before dealing with any 'iffy' passages will pay great dividends.

♦ Are there any elements of 'stylism'? Does style sometimes take precedence over clarity? (See Chapter 9.) Describe your style.

♦ Have you used too many adjectives? Have you used too few?

♦ Have you engaged in any stylistic 'hanky-panky . . . just for the fun of it?' (See Chapter 9.) If so – was it fun?

10. The end

♦ How effective is it?

♦ Is it satisfying – or does it leave the reader feeling stranded and/or disappointed?

- Is it active or reflective?

- Is there a link with the beginning, which brings the story full circle?

- Does it round the story off, make you cry, make you shudder?

- Can you improve it? (See Chapter 5.)

THE END – NO, REALLY...

How much tweaking do you – or can you – do? Knowing when to finish editing is as important as knowing the best way to finish your story, and can be just as much of a problem. Zubin says this is a familiar dilemma for visual artists – there always seems to be another brush stroke or bit of sanding or chiselling you could do. At some point you have to say 'enough' and bring the re-working to an end. In *No Plot – No Problem*, Chris Baty speaks of 'the most awesome catalyst that has ever been unleashed on the worlds of art and commerce . . . a deadline' . As we have discussed in previous chapters, a time limit can indeed focus the mind and speed up production. I have found it also helps with the problem of when to 'walk away'. If I am not restricted by a deadline, I often impose one and bring my rewrites to an end when the time is up – as it is now.

Glossary

Alchemy. Medieval forerunner of chemistry, particularly concerned with the transmutation of base metals into gold or silver. Symbolically a process of transformation.

Archetypes. Ancient images arising from fundamental human experiences. The basic stuff of myths and legends, manifest in universally recognisable roles or concepts, e.g. mother, child, revenge, old age.

Aromatherapy. Balancing of mental and physical energies through the use of essential oils from plants, usually inhaled or applied in diluted form to the skin.

Astrocartography. A branch of astrology which advises on choices of location.

Astrology. The study of the planets in our solar system and the way their energies and movements are reflected in our lives and characters.

Bioenergetics. A body-focused psychotherapy which aims to integrate body and mind. Developed by Dr Alexander Lowen.

Brainwave alteration. Brainwave frequencies are divided into four bands or 'states': *Beta* – highly alert, *Alpha* calmly alert, *Theta* – hypnogogic or meditative, *Delta* – asleep. Brainwaves can be altered to produce these states through relaxation techniques, meditation and pulsing light or sound products designed for the purpose.

Chunking text. Grouping ideas around the page and outlining them, rather than recording them in a linear fashion. This aids both access and memory.

Circadian rhythms. (From the Latin: *circa die* – about a day.) Metabolic rhythms found in most organisms, which generally coincide with the 24-hour day. Additional cycles related to attention span and sleep patterns have been observed in humans.

Decumbiture. An ancient astrological art used by physicians and herbalists to determine the best remedies to prescribe.

De-roling. Performing a series of grounding activities after guided visualisation or role-play in order to re-establish a sense of identity.

Gestalt therapy. A non-interpretative psychotherapy which aims to improve contact with the self and the environment by emphasising awareness.

Guided visualisation. An inner journey guided by scripted instructions.

Horary astrology. A branch of astrology which seeks to answers a specific question by consulting the chart of the moment when the question was asked.

I Ching. An ancient Chinese divination system which draws on the users inner wisdom for help in solving problems. Coins are thrown and a hexagram formed. Every hexagram is associated with an 'answer' in the form of a riddle.

Internal critic. An inner voice which can cause self-doubt and diminish confidence.

Lucid dream. A dream which the dreamer recognises as such and can therefore influence the outcome.

Psyche. Innermost being, essential self, soul, spirit.

Psychotherapy. Sometimes referred to as 'talking therapy'. The non-invasive treatment of neurotic and stress-related disorders through therapeutic relationship with a qualified practitioner.

Repetitive strain syndrome. Physical disorder brought about by repeated use of one body part, e.g. housemaid's knee, tennis elbow. Writers may develop symptoms in wrists, hands and eyes.

Right/left brain. Each side of the brain has its own specialised functions and processes information in its own way. The left side works through logic, the right through intuition. Although they work together for most activities, one side will dominate according to the task.

Runes. An ancient Norse divination system by which marked stones are drawn singly or in spreads in order to gain insight into a difficulty.

S + 7. A technique developed by a group of French experimental novelists. ('S' may stand for *sujet*). A text is selected and its nouns, verbs and adjectives replaced by words which appear seven places away from them in a dictionary.

Shadow self. A person's hidden side, of which they are unaware. Dark in the sense of 'mysterious'. Not necessarily disturbing, but possessing qualities not normally displayed by that person.

Stylism. Pursuit of style at the expense of authenticity and clarity.

Subconscious. The part of the mind which operates below the level of full consciousness.

Synastry. A branch of astrology which compares the chart of two individuals to discover the strengths and weaknesses of their relationship.

Tae Bo. A vigorous fitness routine incorporating a blend of dance, martial arts and boxing moves.

Tarot. A system of 78 cards depicting archetypal characters and experiences, it is the forerunner of modern playing cards, and dates at least from medieval times. Because the mystic symbolism of the tarot makes it an ideal tool for personal growth, it has been adapted to the mythology of many different traditions.

10 x 10. A grid used as the basis for brainstorming 100 'facts' about a given character.

Timed writing. Writing to a preset time without stopping, crossing out or thinking. Used as a warm-up exercise and to by-pass the internal critic.

Tuning in. Becoming still, focusing on a particular issue, and seeking answers in a meditative way.

Word honeycomb. A word association technique starting with 16 words and moving towards a single word in the centre.

Word web. A word association technique which moves outwards from one central word.

Writing backwards. A technique used by writers when it is necessary to set up certain expectations in the reader's mind, e.g. in crime writing, twist-in-the-tale stories and comedy.

References

NON-FICTION BOOKS

The Right-Brain Experience, Marilee Zedenek, (Corgi).

Writing Down the Bones, Natalie Goldberg, (Shambala).

Wild Mind, Natalie Goldberg, (Rider).

Morning Contemplation, Osho, (Boxtree).

Not a Sentimental Journey, Ed. Jo Davis, (Gunbyfield Publishing).

A Writer's Notebook, (Exley Publications).

Dreams, Carl Jung, (Ark Paperbacks).

Dreams and Destiny, (Marshall Cavendish).

The Interpretation of Dreams, Sigmund Freud, (Penguin).

The Elements of Dreamwork, Strephon Kaplan-Williams, (Element Books).

The Dream Lover, Les Peto, (Quantum).

Gestalt Counselling in Action, Petruska Clarkson, (Sage).

No Plot, No Problem, Chris Baty, (Chronicle Books).

Plots Unlimited, Sawyer and Weingarten, (Ashleywilde).

Writing Screenplays that Sell, Michael Hauge, (Elm Tree Books).

Make Your Words Work, Gary Provost, (Writer's Digest Books).

How to Write a Million, Dibell, Scott Card and Turco, (Robinson Publishing).

FICTION

The Waves, Virginia Woolf, (Hogarth Press).

Orlando, Virginia Woolf, (Virago).

To the Lighthouse, Virgina Woolf, (Virago).

Cat's Eye, Margaret Atwood, (Virago).

Republic of Love, Carol Shields, (Flamingo).

Dinner at the Homesick Restaurant, Anne Tyler, (QPD Edition).

If on a winter's night a traveller, Italo Calvino, (Picador).

The Count of Monte Cristo in *Time and the Hunter*, Italo Calvino, (Abacus).

The Curious Incident of the Dog in the Night-time, Mark Haddon, (Vintage).

This Way for the Gas, Ladies and Gentlemen, Tadeusz Borowski, (Penguin).

Behind the Scenes at the Museum, Kate Atkinson, (Black Swan).

Little, Dave Treuer, (Granta).

Pixel Juice, Jeff Noon, (Black Swan).

Still, Adam Thorpe, (QPD Edition).

The October Game in *Long After Midnight*, Ray Bradbury, (Grafton).

Hotel du Lac, Anita Brookner, (Jonathan Cape).

Ride the Iron Horse, Marjorie Darke.

Dr Jekyll and Mr Hyde, Robert Louis Stevenson.

The Lord of the Rings, J.R.R. Tolkein, (Unwin).

The World of Pooh, A.A. Milne, (Methuen).

Alice's Adventures in Wonderland, Lewis Carroll.

TAROT PACKS

The Arthurian Tarot, Caitlin and John Matthews. Illustrator: Miranda Gray, (Thorsons).

The Mythic Tarot, Juliet Sharman-Burke and Liz Greene. Illustrator; Tricia Newell, (Rider).

The Osho-Zen Tarot, Orgo. Commentary/Illustr; Ma Deva Padma, (St Martin's Press).

TAPES

The Creative Fire, Clarissa Pinkola Estes (Sounds True).

COMMENTS AND CONTRIBUTIONS

Marjorie Darke

Jo Davis

Jenny de Garis

Diana Gittins

Alison Harding

Les Peto

Peter Vincent

All tutors and students who have kindly shared their work, experiences and dreams.

Further Reading

ASTROLOGY – BASIC

Understanding Astrology, Sasha Fenton, (Thorsons).
Parker's Astrology, Julia and Derek Parker, (Dorling Kindersley).
Astrology, a Cosmic Science, Isabel M. Hickey, (CRCS Publications).
Mythic Astrology, Ariel Guttman and Kenneth Johnson, (Llewellyn Pub.).

ASTROLOGY – SPECIALISED

Horary Astrology, Dr Marc Edmund Jones, (Aurora Press).
Relating, Liz Greene, (Thorsons).
The Development of the Personality, Liz Greene and Howard Sasportas, (Penguin).
Synastry, Ronald Davison, (Aurora Press).

DREAMWORK

Dream Sharing, Robin Shohet, (Crucible).
Lucid Dreaming, Stephen LaBerge and Howard Rheingold, (Ballantine Books).
What Your Dreams Can Teach You, Alex Lukeman, (Llewellyn Publications).

GENERAL REFERENCE

A Dictionary of Symbols, Tom Chetwynd, (Paladin).
The Oxford Companion to the Mind, Ed. Richard L. Gregory, (OUP).

Consciousness Explained, Daniel C. Dennett, (The Penguin Press).

The Elements of the I Ching, Stephen Karcher, (Element Books).

Tarot for Beginners, Kristyna Arcarti, (Hodder and Stoughton).

VISUALISATION

At a Journal Workshop, Ira Progoff, (Tarcher, Putnam).

Awareness, John O. Stevens, (Eden Grove).

Life Choices and Life Changes Through Imagework, Diana Glouberman, (Unwin).

Walking Through Walls, Will Parfitt, (Element Books).

What We May Be, Piero Ferrucci, (Turnstone Press).

WRITING

Becoming a Writer, Dorothea Brande, (Macmillan).

Comedy Writing Secrets, Melvin Helitzer, (Writer's Digest Books).

The Craft of Writing Poetry, Alison Chisolm, (Alison and Busby).

Creative Writing, Adele Ramet, (How To Books).

Fast Fiction, Roberta Allen, (Story Press).

How to Write Comedy, Brad Ashton, (Elm Tree Books).

Plot and Structure, James Scott Bell, (Writer's Digest).

Story, Robert McKee, (Methuen).

The Art of Fiction, David Lodge, (Penguin).

Twenty Master Plots and How to Build Them, Ronald B. Tobias, (Piatkus).

Word Power, Julian Birkett, (A & C Black).

Write for Life, Nicki Jackowska, (Element).

The Writer's Guide to Getting Published, Chriss McCallum, (How To Books).

Writing Past Dark, Bonnie Friedman, (Harper Perennial).

Zen in the Art of Writing, Ray Bradbury, (Joshua Odell).

Useful Addresses and Websites

ASTROLOGICAL SOFTWARE

Astrocalc UK, 67, Peascroft Road, Hemel Hempstead, Herts HP3
    8ER.
Roy Gillett Consultants, 32, Glynswood, Camberley, Surrey GU15
    1HU.
Midheaven Bookshop, 396, Caledonian Road, London N1 1DN.
World of Wisdom, 20 Potters Lane, New Barnet, Herts EN5 5BH.

ASTROLOGY CORRESPONDENCE COURSES

The English Huber School, PO Box 118, Knutsford, Cheshire
    WA16 8TG.
The Mayo School, Alvana Gardens, Tregavethan, Truro, Cornwall
    TR4 9EN.

EXERCISE/LIFESTYLE VIDEOS AND SOFTWARE

Visual Entertainment, FREEPOST LON8942, London SE1 7YZ.
http://RSIGuard.com
http://WorkPace.com
http://PrimeMover.com

PERSONAL GROWTH PRODUCTS AND WEBSITES

(The following are suppliers of products mentioned in this book.
Typing 'Personal Growth Products' into your search engine will,
of course, list many more.)

LifeTools, Freepost SK 1852, Macclesfield SK10 2YE or
www.lifetools.com

New World Music, Harmony House, Hillside Road, Bungay,
Suffolk NR35 1RX or www.newworldmusic.com

Novapro www.braintuner.com/novapro

Osho Purnima Distribution, Greenwise, Vange Park Rd, Basildon,
Essex SS16 5LA or www.omweb.com/osho or
www.oshohereandnow.com

Photosonix www.toolsforwellness.com

SCRIPTS

Book City, 308 N. San Fernando Blvd. Dept.101, Burbank CA
91502 USA.

Faber and Faber Ltd, 3, Queen Square, London WC1N 3AU

TAPES

BBC Radio, Broadcasting House, London W1A 1AA.

Sounds True, 735 Walnut Street, Colorado 80302, USA.

WRITERS' SOFTWARE

Dreampack for Writers (Shareware) www.dreampack.com

www.newnovelist.com

www.literarymachine.com

Plots Unlimited and Storybase www.ashleywilde.com

www.WriteQuickly.com

www.writesparks.com

WRITERS' WEBSITES

e-mail writing courses http:writingbliss.com

e-writing http:ewritersplace.com

Get Writing www.bbc.co.uk/dna/getwriting

Getting published online www.travel-wise.com/50online_listings

Recommended books for fiction writers www.noveladvice.com
UK Fiction Markets www.garyhayden.co.uk
www.writersdock.co.uk
www.writerspace.com

Index